C000214459

the
Ripple
effect

How surprisingly **small** changes in
mindset can make **big** things happen

DAVID J HARKIN

The Ripple Effect
ISBN 978-1-912300-64-8
eISBN 978-1-912300-65-5

Published in 2022 by SRA Books
Printed in the UK

© Halphabet 2022

The right of David J. Harkin to be identified as the author of this work has been asserted in accordance with the Copyright, Designs and Patents Act 1988.

A CIP record of this book is available from the British Library.

All rights reserved. No part of this book may be reproduced, stored in a retrieval system, or transmitted in any form or by any means, electronic, mechanical, photocopying, recording or otherwise, without the prior written permission of the copyright holder.

No responsibility for loss occasioned to any person acting or refraining from action as a result of any material in this publication can be accepted by the author or publisher.

Contents

*To my gorgeous Jenny, Toby, Harry (and bump),
I will be forever in your debt for everything you
do for me. I love you to pieces, and this book is
dedicated to you*

xxx

Introduction

Why write a book?

I never thought I would actually write a book, let alone a book with 40,000 words in it. Growing up, I never disliked English, but just always found that I could vocalise myself better than writing words down on a piece of paper. However, as I've got older, I've often found the urge to get to my laptop and write down a quick blog which has come into my head after being out on a run, a walk with the dog or a drive to work.

From these blogs have come comments, questions, observations and a thirst from just my immediate network to learn a little more about some of the things that were in my head. Keynote requests would come in from organisations, corporates and conference events to build on something I wrote and in the end, they formed the basis of two TEDx talks I was privileged to have had the opportunity to deliver in 2018 and 2020.

Alongside these interactions with my network, I also became a dad. I'm fortunate enough to be married to my gorgeous Jenny and have our beautiful children. Many of the things that I was writing about – attitude, mentality, innovation, etc. – I do hope at some point in the future that they might read and maybe take something away for their own personal lives and careers, whatever they choose to do. It's surprising that sometimes opportunities to pass on lessons don't easily appear. With all of the knowledge and experience we accumulate over a lifetime, it's a shame, but at least some of the core things that I believe are important to living a life that creates positive ripples are now within this book for them to read in the future.

With the writing, the TEDx talks and becoming a dad, I began to think that maybe, just maybe I could bring my ideas into one place: a book that is timeless, helpful to my children in the future, but also helpful to readers right now. Writing a book takes a lot of energy and time, so although I'm keen for my children to enjoy it, I hope it has a much bigger ripple than just them.

The Ripple Effect is a book that is for the self-improver, the ambitious type, the individual who wants to make their mark, no matter where they are in their life. A book that is easy to read, doesn't take months to complete, has some interesting personal stories that the reader can relate to but, importantly, also some simple and useful tips that any individual can pick up and implement – no matter if you're a student, apprentice or graduate; are unemployed, an entrepreneur, manager, director or CEO; are retired, a politician, a teacher... or even my mum and dad!

I've always personally enjoyed self-improvement books. Ones that make you think, ones that give you something really tangible to go and implement in your daily lives. But sometimes they can be a little overcomplicated, loaded with scientific theory and random case studies.

I've attempted to keep *The Ripple Effect* straightforward, easy to read, and give you something to take away by drawing on my own experience as an intrapreneur and then becoming an entrepreneur.

An intrapreneur is someone who acts like an entrepreneur within an organisation or a business and this is what I found myself doing in the corporate space. I was always taking risks, always generating and developing new ideas and always looking to push relentlessly. Upon reading an article about this new word 'intrapreneur', I realised that that was what I was. I also knew at some point the boundaries set around me in the corporate world would lead to me breaking free and becoming an entrepreneur, which I've been now since the age of 28. My experiences on both sides of the fence, among other experiences, will hopefully be insightful to the readers of this book.

My goal throughout has been to make this an enjoyable and impactful book. I've always believed in the power of trying to create memorable moments for individuals in my work, but I'm conscious that in a book, if a reader can actually walk away with even one thing that will help them, then that is actually a success.

I've tried to imagine what you will say to your friends, family or colleagues about this book and hope it might be one of the personal stories, an interesting quote or even one of the key takeaways and tips at the end of each level which I know will hit home with many of you.

I know this because over the years when I've shared these tips with people, I've always had the reaction of 'Wow, that's a good tip' or 'I've never thought about it like that', or 'David, have you ever thought about sharing these in a book?' I'm hoping you all agree with these nice comments from friends, family and colleagues in the past and enjoy the tips at the end of each level.

The structure of the chapters has been thought through at length with key sections, top tips and reflections. Each could be read as a standalone, but actually when they're strung together, the flow (in my opinion) is clear, as they build on one another to make sure the reader at the end of the level has a good understanding of many key areas that I believe are vital if you wish to create positive ripples in your life.

Rather than chapters, you'll see I refer to *levels*. Level 1 really introduces the whole theory of *The Ripple Effect*, while Level 8 is reflective about the future. Levels 2–7 in between are focused, specialised areas for you to consider to help you in certain areas. Naturally, I feel they join up nicely, leading on to one another, but also don't feel afraid to jump back and forward in the book if there is something you need or want to immediately focus on.

To every single one of you who've taken the time to read this book – thank you. It's such a privilege to be able to enter your lives for a few hours as you consume the words that I've spent so long writing and I truly hope you enjoy the book. Please always feel free to reach out to me on social media with your comments, questions, follow-ups, etc. and I will come back to every one of you as soon as I can.

To every member of my team (in particular Tara for your support with this book) and to the editors who have helped me along the way with additional research, reading the words that I've written and giving feedback, and who have helped me with thinking about the structure and the approach, thank you. Without your energy, enthusiasm and, indeed, your patience around me on a daily basis, none of what we achieve together would be possible.

To all of my network, friends and family who have

supported me throughout my career, including you Mum and Dad and indeed my in-laws – thank you. As part of my ripple effect, you've all played a part in my journey to date and I will be forever grateful for your support, your help, your inspiration and love throughout the years. Some of you might read this and realise a story or two is about you! Sorry I never asked, but they're all nice stories for the readers to enjoy.

To my children – you've been a constant inspiration to me, despite your chaos. You inspire me to keep going, to keep making my impact on the planet and to keep building a family home which you can thrive in. I hope when you read this you take from it what you want and each of you goes and makes positive ripples in whatever you want to do. Just make sure you stay kind!

Finally, to my Jenny – without you, none of what I do would be possible. Your love makes me the luckiest man in the world and this book has so much of your inspiration all over it. You've given me ideas throughout every level, re-read, edited, proposed changes, pushed me to make this the best book I can. You've made sacrifices for me, so I could have the time to write this book: thank you for this and thank you for everything you do for me and our family. This book is dedicated to you and our children.

Over to you the reader now, to consume these levels and start making positive ripples in your life way beyond what you can imagine. I've never met anyone who doesn't have an amazing imagination and each of us has the ability to go and change the world in tiny, small or big ways on a daily basis. But to achieve this we must have the skills and the belief. I hope this book gives you the belief you can make ripples and some skills to help you go and do that.

Let's get started.

Level 1

Creating Ripples

If you throw a pebble into a pond it will make ripples. Some will make small ripples and others will make bigger, longer-lasting ones, but every pebble will make some sort of a ripple. We all make ripples every day that impact our families, friends, colleagues, clients and whoever we come into contact with. A positive ripple can change someone's day or even their life and, on the flip side, a negative ripple can have a toxic impact on those around us. We can and must control those ripples which we as individuals and leaders make on a daily basis.

The 'ripple effect' has a distinct meaning in business: 'the notion that a single action has an effect over several different entities'.[1] In this level we are going to look at how you can cause a ripple effect across your

---

1 https://smallbusiness.chron.com/ripple-effect-business-22463.html

network. I will address the good, the bad and the ugly of influencing because there are many examples of how influencing can have both positive and negative effects. However, we must start with realising that the ripples we make are all down to us and there are things we can do to help us make as many positive ripples as possible on a daily basis.

Survival time

I was in my mid-twenties when I began to really think about the ripple effect. I was working my way up through a technology giant, earning my first real income, making friends and having a good time. I was doing well; I had more energy than most and relentlessly pushed for more each day. Yet something didn't feel right. It took time to dawn on me, but I realised I was 'corporate claustrophobic'. This is my way of describing how I was feeling in my career: I felt trapped. I was just 25 years old.

A pivotal turning point for me came when I was attending a conference with over 400 employees and we spent five days watching dozens of presentations. Apart from being incredibly bored at times because the presentations were not engaging, I realised that I was a tiny ant in a massive organisation. My ability to really affect its future, change its direction and have a wider positive impact was next to zero per cent within this particular organisation. My wife had once joked when looking out of a plane about how it made her think we were just all ants on the planet, but that was exactly how I felt in my corporate life when I realised I had very little ability to create ripples. Without the ability to create real impact, I was claustrophobic. I needed to change and that's when I decided to jump into becoming an entrepreneur.

More accurately, I didn't just jump without a decent idea or plan. There's an image of entrepreneurs that they have to risk it all from day one but more often than not that's not the case – *and shouldn't be the case*. I had to put in the groundwork to form my first business. I devoted time outside of work, at the weekends, on my holidays, to think hard and develop the idea and go and win some initial clients. It meant that when I did leap, I had reduced the risk of a failure (and that of being completely skint). I had worked out my 'survival time', i.e. how much cash and time I had to make it really work before giving it up or redirecting my energy somewhere else. I always say this to new entrepreneurs: *make sure you build as much survival time into your business at the start by whatever means necessary*. Sometimes, the best thing you can do is do a job on the side, so you're not counting pennies every day!

For me, I decided to create enough survival time by a combination of going from full time to part time with my day job, saving up as much as I could in that period, and then making a bigger decision with my wife to remortgage the house to free up some capital. I knew I needed at least 18–24 months to make it work as we were about to leap into a completely new sector for us. The remortgage was a relatively easy decision with my wife, but strangely, I felt I needed the emotional approval from my father too, which I received straight away. I explained what I wanted to do, my logic behind it and that I wanted to have no regrets. If it didn't work after this period, I would be young enough to jump back into the corporate world. His response to me, which I will never forget was, 'I guess it's like a real-life MBA. The lessons you will learn from your own investment into this will put you in good stead for the rest of your life.

This will make you more valuable in the corporate world or your next venture. Just promise me, if it's not working you don't get too stubborn and lose it all.' I promised him and the rest was history. Those steps bought us the time we needed and the emotional support was no doubt just as valuable to me as a newbie entrepreneur.

The reason I encourage entrepreneurs to think about their survival time is because I know good ideas can become bad ideas if rushed or if you don't give yourself enough time to see them fully develop. If you can build yourself as much survival time as possible, and not be too stubborn to alter your idea, more often than not you'll end up developing your idea into a business concept that could be sustainable. For me, from the initial idea and that moment of feeling claustrophobic to making that 'leap' was actually a two-year period, but at the end of those two years I was confident about making it. Since then, I have learned a huge amount about myself, but the biggest thing I've learned is that daily I actually make thousands of ripples. Some good and some not so good.

Different ripples

I first noticed the 'not so good' when the business was beginning to establish itself and I was being pulled from pillar to post, which is exhausting. You're winning your clients, you're involved in the delivery of your services, you're hiring your first employees, while also trying to be a good spouse, parent, family member and friend. Exhaustion can lead to lots of different behaviours – one of them being occasionally snappy or not in the best of moods. It was when I was in exhaustion mode and speaking to my team that I realised that it was having a knock-on effect on them and creating ripples – but not the right kind. If I am in a bad mood, I might be a little short, a little snappy, or a tiny bit less polite. To those on the other end, it would affect their own mood. If they were in a good place, I would have just changed that. If they were in a negative place themselves, I had no doubt I made them a little more negative. On the flip side, when I felt like I was on fire, invincible or in my ideal flow state, this had the ability to create positive ripples, boost the morale of those around me and take the productivity of my team to a new level, sometimes for days. This is when I realised that every day I was making ripples and no matter what my mood was, I had to control it because it wouldn't necessarily benefit the people around me or the business that I was trying to create.

I think it is important to note that this isn't just for leaders to be aware of but everyone. I keenly observe within my team the individuals who make positive and negative ripples. It won't be a surprise that those who create positive ripples grab my attention more often than those creating negative ripples, who get focus in the wrong way. Creating ripples is something all of us need to be aware of as we go through life and progress at work and at home, becoming role models to employees and potentially younger family members.

The art of influencing

A good place to start when thinking about how to create positive ripples is realising the power of influence. Why is this a good place to start? Because if you can positively influence those around you, your ripples will last longer and go further; those you influence will in turn influence others with your messages, ideas or indeed just your energy.

There are dozens of books available on how to influence people and there are many methods that people tout as being the best for influencing people, some of these include:

➤ being a leader (not a 'boss')
➤ empowering people
➤ connecting with others' emotions
➤ respecting other people's opinions.

Whatever the tool you use, the aim is essentially the same: you want to influence because you're trying to encourage them to see or hear your vision, the benefits of your business or indeed of you as a leader or employer. Whatever it is you are offering, you will need to influence people to want it and you must realise that 'influencing' isn't a bad thing. It doesn't mean being 'salesy', manipulative or pushy; it's about using some of those methods listed above to get the best out of your team members and win new customers. *Why wouldn't you want to do that?*

One great example of having to influence someone, and one we've all had to do at some point, is the interview process. At each stage during the interview process you need to influence someone. First you need your application to be considered and reviewed. You need to be invited to the interview and then, at this point, it really is down to you to do your best to influence the decision-makers to make them feel like you're the best person for the job. If you don't, someone else will. I often hear of people who feel like they've missed out on a dream job, but when I ask them about their preparation or what stories they told in their interview, they often didn't prepare well enough or were too shy to tell the stories of their strengths and successes because they felt they would appear to be arrogant or boastful. But an interview process is *exactly* the time to influence those people and be proud of your achievements, because if you don't tell them, how will they ever know?

I remember someone I used to mentor telling me he was frustrated that he hadn't landed his dream job. He was a good person, had the right attitude and had the skills, so I said, 'Let's do a dive into your CV and see if you can highlight some aspects.' After a few questions about his background and hobbies outside of work, I found that probably the most impressive thing about him wasn't even on his CV or he thought wasn't relevant to bring up in his interview.

Approximately ten years prior to our conversation, he had spotted an opportunity on his street to make money for charity with his father by collecting Christmas trees. They both agreed that for £10 they would take away the tree and donate the money to the local hospice. Momentum grew from year to year and they expanded from one street to the next, then finally from one town to the next. They ended up forming a partnership with the local council to help with the removal of the trees and mass collect money for the charity they supported. The culmination of all this hard work led them to raise £250,000+ in that period. Quite an amazing story, but nowhere to be seen on his CV or he didn't think it was relevant to bring up. To me, this showed empathy, dedication, organisation and creativity among a long list of skills. I then gave him a telling off and told him never to let that one slip again, get it on that CV and be proud of what he's done. *He then went and got the next job he applied for...*

If we flip back to the list I shared with you about methods to influence, one of them is based around emotion. It surprised me early on in my career to learn that 95 per cent of purchasing decisions are subconscious and are based on emotion and feeling.[2] I'm sure there are times which spring to mind when you wanted to buy something because you *had a feeling* about it; it wasn't necessarily something you could put your finger on, but it felt 'right' and your gut instinct was telling you something. Maybe it gave you a sense of happiness, self-worth or belonging. It is those emotional feelings I want you to be aware of when it comes to your life, professionally and personally too because this can have a profound impact on the loved ones you share your days with.

Without being aware of these emotions and tapping into them, you can't make a connection and you can't influence effectively. Of course, you can't know everything about a person's subconscious and how they might feel or respond to things; sometimes we might get it wrong – remember that in business 'you win some, you lose some'. However, you can improve your chances. Try putting yourself in their shoes, for instance. Think about the person you're trying to influence, whether they're an employee or a potential customer, and think about what's important to them and what they value. How can you tap into that? To fully appreciate your own worth in whatever you do, you need to identify who you are targeting and why; then the right people come along: *visualise to materialise.*

---

2 www.inc.com/logan-chierotti/harvard-professor-says-95-of-purchasing-decisions-are-subconscious.html

Using your emotions to influence

Even the word 'emotion' can generate different reactions in people. I used to say, 'I'm not emotional', which is a stupid thing to say, because we all are. Emotion, and being emotional, is what gives us our drive, the fire in our bellies, and it fuels us daily. I normally find my emotions high when a situation is affecting my family, or indeed the business, and a human instinct kicks in to protect those that I love and the things that I'm passionate about.

It wasn't very long ago that people used to feel embarrassed talking about emotions, even acknowledging them; it was often seen as being weak, especially in business. As time has gone on, I feel like we all seem to be getting better at recognising and accepting that we experience a range of emotions and these don't go away when we come to work. I salute these changes in trends, but a trend which must follow in conjunction with this is for all of us to become better listeners as more people speak up. In recent years, I've sometimes attempted to speak more about my emotions, but sometimes I have found those listening want to solve everything that I'm talking about when sometimes the best thing they can do is listen.

Using your emotions to create ripples is very powerful, but if you do find yourself on the receiving end of someone sharing their emotions, please stop and truly listen to them.

Motivation is a power

It's long been a mantra in the business world that you leave your emotions at the office door and put your work face on, but is this realistic or even desirable? If you want a good ripple effect, influencing your customers is one thing, but *it must start with your teams*. Employee retention needs to encompass incentives and motivation. Motivation is one of those intrinsic values that is hard to quantify but it's our job as leaders to use those emotional tools to engage people and increase those positive ripples. Emotions can be positive too and drive us forward, although we aren't machines, so we have to allow for some down days or moments too.

Occasionally, I do wonder to myself if people really want emotional leaders. Of course, emotion can show you're passionate about something and inspire people, but if you wear your heart on your sleeve too much, it could spread worry. Leaders do tread a fine line. A healthy balance is required and you need to pick and choose what you do leave at the door of the office and what you bring in. Let me give you a good example.

I once was preparing one of my businesses for a new venture and, as a result, required private equity backing. Once term sheets were secured, I thought we would be in a great place; however, in this situation our private equity firm couldn't keep to their side of the bargain. But to my own team, including lots of new hires, which this funding was for, I couldn't let on what was happening behind the scenes. I needed my team focused on the product and launch in hand. The slightest suggestion from me to the team that things were challenging behind the scenes could and would have had negative ripples on what the business was trying to achieve. I had to control this emotion when I spoke to them. It was the right decision and, three months after launch, after the funding situation improved and we became revenue generating; it was only then that I felt I could tell them and that I could be emotional and vulnerable in front of them, without creating negative ripples. By controlling this, the knock-on effect was a sense of respect from my team, an appreciation of what I had done and a new focus from everyone to seize the opportunity in front of us.

Verbal and non-verbal communication

Another important thing to think about, especially with regard to emotion as a way of influencing, is our verbal and non-verbal communication. As a leader, you can really show your strength in this area if you can home in on what it is that gets the best out of people. Many of you will know the difference already, but to be clear, non-verbal communication includes:[3]

- ➤ tone of voice
- ➤ rate and volume of speech
- ➤ how we articulate our words
- ➤ rhythm, intonation and stress placed on words
- ➤ facial expression
- ➤ the amount of eye contact we make
- ➤ gestures/touch
- ➤ body language and posture.

Staggeringly, only seven per cent of what we say in words conveys our meaning, *fifty-five per cent is from body language* and the rest is *tone of voice*.[4] That's a huge

---

3 www.workplacestrategiesformentalhealth.com/mmhm/pdf/full_communicating_0.pdf
4 www.rightattitudes.com/2008/10/04/7-38-55-rule-personal-communication/

difference between verbal and non-verbal! Facts like this have been a big influence on my keynote speaking. I make sure I control everything that takes place on the stage, not just the words I speak. I think hard about my appearance, about the energy in my voice, even the power of a pause. I control as much as I can that affects my body language to make sure that the words I say are complemented and reinforced by everything else to get my meaning and points across.

Just to pause on the appearance aspect: I think it's key for confidence. Let's be clear on this: this isn't about dedicating hours at the gym to get ripped and walk on the stage looking like a model; it is about wearing clothes that make you feel confident and comfortable and gain respect from the audience. For example, I wouldn't walk onto a TED stage or deliver a keynote in flip flops; some might pull it off, but that's not me. It's distracting from the words that I'm saying, as the audience would be thinking about my foot attire more than the words I speak. Equally, I very rarely would walk onto a stage and present in a tie and a jacket – why? Because for me, that makes me feel hot; it can also block my vocal cords, having an impact on my voice. My most common appearance now is dark jeans, smart trainers and a white T-shirt or shirt. Wearing this outfit is when I'm comfortable, smart enough to not be distracting to the audience, and when I feel at my most confident. Fortunately, since moving from the corporate world, I've been lucky to drop the shirt-and-tie combination more often than not and I relish the freedom a smart T-shirt brings. All I would say here is don't underestimate the importance of appearance when on stage – this is something you can control, so control it.

Over the years, we've begun to see some notable

individuals such as Steve Jobs, Barack Obama, Marc Zuckerberg and Simon Cowell decide to be consistent with what they wear. Find something comfortable and stick with it. It's been a smart move for these individuals as it's become part of their brand and allows the listeners to focus on their words.

Unfortunately this doesn't seem to be the same for women, where the scrutiny is just unfair and the media needs to stop it. I remember when Theresa May was having a difficult time as the UK prime minister and after coughing her way from a speech at a political party conference, she had the courage to come back on stage the next day. However, the news channels just zoomed in on her foot attire, smart high-heeled, zebra-styled shoes. I couldn't help thinking if this was the other way round, they would have never done that. I hope in the years ahead, scrutiny for all sexes, but particularly women, will only be on what people say and not what they wear.

If I bring this back to the other seven per cent element – the actual words – this isn't something I ignore. To me, there is no point looking great, moving great, dominating on a stage and then letting slip on the verbal element. I've always felt speaking to an audience, no matter the size, to be a privilege and an opportunity to inspire. Whether or not you're speaking for a few minutes or an hour, for that time you've got the opportunity to engage with an audience, who in turn are giving up their time to listen. It's my duty to own that moment, use the time on stage and get the words I want across in the best possible way. It's why I prepare so highly on all fronts for any external speaking engagement. So although it's only seven per cent, it's still crucial and there are ways that you can maximise it.

Give and take

There are other ways of influencing. Dr Robert Cialdini wrote that there are six factors behind influence in his book *Influence: The Psychology of Persuasion*. The first he refers to is *reciprocity* and he explains how powerful it is to give a gift. The basic idea is that people are more likely to give something when they've already been given something. He cites the restaurant trade and even the simple giving of a chocolate or a mint at the end of a meal could increase tips from diners by three per cent, but having the waiting staff add a nice comment directly to the diners, this increased to 23 per cent! You might need more than a mint as a gift, but the principle is the same in any form of business: *find a way to recognise and thank your customers and colleagues*. A thank you goes a long way, but a gift goes even further.

It's important to not only make strong impressions at the end of a service or engagement with a client, to leave that 'feel good factor', but also to create positive impressions from the start.

Before the influx of online shopping took over, the high street was the go-to place for everything anyone needed. Relying heavily on footfall, it was important to retailers that all customers had a positive experience so they would tell all their friends. Customers would also tell people they knew about bad experiences, to as many as nine or more people, which would in itself cause a ripple effect, but of the negative kind. The detrimental effect this could have on a business could spell the end of it. The same is true of online shopping; it is subject to the same kind of ripples, and the numbers are staggeringly high. Ninety-four per cent of consumers have avoided a company after reading a review, and four out of five consumers have decided not to buy a recommended product after reading a negative review.[5] That's a lot of ripples! We've also seen the length of time customers are prepared to stay on a website before being bored and leaving decline in recent years. It's unlikely people will give more than 10-20 seconds before they work out if they want to spend any longer on it. It's crucial in those first few seconds to show value and grab that potential client.

Beyond the world of commerce, it's no different to meeting real people. Forbes once featured an article claiming that it would take eight positive encounters with an individual to turn around a first bad impression, and this doesn't surprise me.[6] If people walk into an interview and can't do their top button up and put their tie on properly, I'm not interested. I'm sorry, I'm not. To me, the first impression is that this person is untidy and if they can't get changed for an interview, how will they be with the team or our clients? They might be a rocket scientist, but the first impression is not a good one and that's the end of that.

It's also a bit like dating, and I'll tread carefully on this topic! But it's often in those first few seconds of a date (if my memory serves me correctly!) that your first impressions are set. Am I interested in getting to know this person more or am I already thinking about the bill? We all know this is the case. Luckily with my wife, I knew she liked to be surprised, so I decided to not take her on a dinner date, but we went for a drum lesson and drinks

---

5 https://medium.com/revain/why-are-customer-reviews-so-important-185b915d4e5d
6 www.forbes.com/sites/work-in-progress/2015/02/10/the-do-over-how-to-correct-a-bad-first-impression

instead. She showed me no intention of wanting to learn the drums, but I thought it would make her smile and it did – we had fun and the rest was history.

Nurturing your network

One area we can't overlook when it comes to creating ripples and influencing people is 'nurturing your network'. Why? Because your network can double or even triple your own personal ripples to your contacts' own connections and networks. If your positive ripples affect an individual it will have a domino effect because they will go and make ripples in their own circles of influence on that day. For example, if I spoke to a team member late on a Friday and thanked them for their efforts that week before the weekend, that individual would bounce into the weekend with their friends and family with energy. The empowerment that I had passed from me to them would then ripple into nice waves over the weekend. These people might not work for me, but they're within my extended network and it's a good example of why nurturing your network is important.

For me this is about trust and reciprocity – I get to know people and they get to know me. I also benefit because I give back. People buy from people and that again reinforces the emotion behind why we buy and why those intangible connections exist. The great thing about this is that we all connect differently. Don't make the mistake of thinking this is about you connecting with anyone and everyone; it's about building and growing with the 'right' people – the ones you connect with most.

One of the most important pieces of advice for anyone networking, whether a stalwart or a newbie, is to *listen*. It's not about talking about what *you* do, but listening to what others do. Be patient and wait for your moment to put yourself out there for them. It might mean a leap of faith but, having listened to them, you know what it is they need, and forewarned is forearmed. As these connections build, you may notice that people start saying similar things about you, and you need to take on that feedback to find a way to connect with more people. Be warned, however: being self-aware can be painful, and sometimes you may discover things you don't like. But if we can build upon feedback, it's an important tool in growing ourselves, being better influencers and creating more ripples in the right ponds.

Reach far and wide

How wide is the reach of your network? It's great to rely on friends and family, especially when starting out or when you need a boost or perhaps a dose of reality, but you might want to create ripples far and wide. With amazing platforms such as LinkedIn, the world is at your fingertips – you don't even have to leave the house. Some believe that instead of six degrees of separation, it's now notably fewer. Facebook believes it's 3.57 degrees of separation, while others think it's now only two.[7] That makes for a much smaller world than we ever imagined – think just how much of an influence we've been having. And the population is growing – just consider the possibilities that exist! Your ripples need to be constant and have to move in the right direction to realise your potential. This is what you need to tap into for your business or organisation and your personal brand.

---

7 www.digitaldoughnut.com/articles/2017/august/6-degrees-of-separation-is-now-2

You might feel like a small fish in a big pond, but we are all in the same position. It's how you use your network and your mentality that will help you stand out from the crowd and be recognised – it's a cliché but so true. There is a sea of brands, faces and marketing slogans, and that's where your ripples come in. It might be from one pebble at a time, but you build traction, and you will get noticed.

In a way, we're lucky in the 21st century how networking has expanded beyond the physical connections we make to the digital ones, which can be more powerful. I think when talking to peers or young people, we must remind them that both are actually equally important and demystify the fact, which is still drummed home in some circles, that networking is about the ability to walk into a room with confidence and give your business card out to everyone. This isn't the case anymore. It's about knowing how to build a network where you can help those within it and they can help you. Smart networking can help everyone beyond what you can imagine.

Build your brand

A big part of growing your network is establishing a connection and rapport with people. How many times have you seen people selling what they do but there is no energy or enthusiasm – no connection? Is that who you would buy from? *I hate the direct messages I get from people on LinkedIn listing their services with no passion or thought.* Sometimes the brand might speak for itself, and once you have bought into a brand you might stay loyal to it, but that brand *came from a person* and grew from there. Remember, *people buy from people at the end of the day!*

As I have 'CEO' in my title, I get hundreds of LinkedIn

messages on a monthly basis – many of them are people reaching out trying to sell things. Ninety-nine per cent of them are rubbish. Long lists of products and services they have, with zero effort to build rapport or find a common reason to speak beyond work. The one per cent who do ten minutes' research before messaging me are normally the ones who grab my attention. If they grab my attention I always respond with a 'thank you' or 'no, thank you'. If they don't, they get deleted as I don't want to waste a second of my life on someone reaching out to me and making no effort. If they spell my company name wrong, or even get my own name wrong, I'm very quick to block them too! I was even called Melonie once...

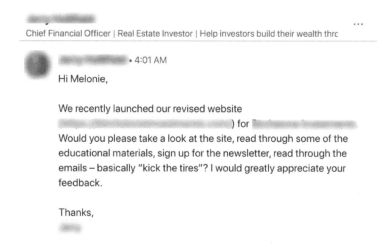

Let's move on to the point where you've established your reputation and built a network that trusts you: is that the end of the story? Definitely not. The work continues and you keep moving forward. This has got to be driven from the top and that's why we talk about people being leaders and not bosses. A leader has the ability to keep that trust and build relationships with customers and staff, which will stand you in good stead for the future. It is your job to maintain that influence and this is where your team, and your network, comes in. They are representatives of your values and, without people representing you, you don't really have an influence. So, *lead by example and create your personal brand*; this is what will help you to create ripples which will spread far and wide, and keep your network growing.

The six, or rather two, degrees of separation allow you to mix in circles you wouldn't normally have access to. But remember, although a large network is great, you need to use it wisely and make sure you're connecting with the right people too. Think strategically and ask yourself who the ideal person is you want to work with. Do you have a specific name in mind for who you need a conversation with? Ask and the network can deliver – that person is only two steps away! If the network can't deliver, perhaps you haven't put the hard work in first, building that trust, that relationship. What more can you do? Remember, it takes more than words to build a network. We can all tell people what we do, but we know our words only count for seven per cent of communication. Showing people is where the trust starts to come into its own. Lead by example, show people that you're someone they can trust and connect with. You only need one person to buy into you and your personal brand and it grows from there, but only as long as you maintain your influence.

You probably remember people who've influenced you the most in your life – maybe a teacher at school, something you watched or read or on a podcast you heard. We don't always need a lot; just one small quote or speech can be enough. This can be a driving force and motivation that in turn helps us influence others.

Hopefully you now realise the impact your influence can have. Every day, you can find ways to inspire people! Build your personal brand and use your networking channels to share relevant and interesting information, and be the expert people turn to.

Please also remember that ripples are made beyond just physical and real interactions with people, but also done virtually and via social media. Virtually, we can make ripples from the moment our online meetings start, and on social media every single post we make can get a reaction, whether it's a like, dislike, comment or a share. It's actually these tools which can explode your ripples further than you can imagine. It's one to think about as you continue to read through this book. Creating ripples must start with an appreciation of your real-life network, but consider the digital network too.

Bringing it all together

Let's remind ourselves of what the positives of creating ripples are:

- ➤ Your ideas and thoughts can spread quickly through positive ripples.
- ➤ If powerful, they can also spread far.
- ➤ People will gravitate towards you and your visions.
- ➤ You begin to appreciate that small conversations and moments count.
- ➤ You can also achieve your personal goals.

So, where could you start in embracing this philosophy of creating ripples?

Top tip: Calculate your 'Ripple Number'

It's time for a top tip to drum this level home. Have you ever thought about how far your ripples could actually go and the number of people they could affect?

My first tip for you would be to try and work it out on a typical day and create your rough Ripple Number. The first thing to do is calculate those people you directly encounter; this is Ripple Wave 1:

- ➤ people you live with and those they encounter on a daily basis
- ➤ people you work with and those they encounter on a daily basis
- ➤ people you randomly meet on a daily basis
- ➤ people you connect with through the use of social media or your phone.

For me, it roughly works like this:

- ➤ wife
- ➤ kids
- ➤ family
- ➤ friends
- ➤ employees
- ➤ clients
- ➤ users/audience
- ➤ suppliers
- ➤ neighbours/random encounters
- ➤ social media following.

If I put a rough number on each of the above right now, it quickly adds up:

- ➤ Wife – 1 – *just the one wife, Jenny*
- ➤ Kids – 2 – *two young lads, Harry and Toby*
- ➤ Family – 17 – *just direct family; never a day goes by without a message*
- ➤ Friends – 300+ – *probably interact on social media and touch base with a few*
- ➤ Employees/contractors – 40 – *will no doubt see me on a Zoom or two!*
- ➤ Clients – 12 – *I might have a dozen or so client meetings conversations in a day*
- ➤ Presentation – 250+ – *probably a daily pitch or speech to an audience*
- ➤ Suppliers – 3 – *no doubt an email or two with a key supplier*
- ➤ Neighbours – 2 – *I do love a conversation with the neighbours*
- ➤ Social media following – 10,000+ – *I'm active on Twitter/LinkedIn.*

This would make my first wave Ripple Number 10,627. Let's round it down to 10,000 people. These 10,000 connections could (not always) be impacted by something I say, the way that I react, a post I make or even just a piece of body language. Something I do or say could impact their lives.

To give you an example, it's not unreasonable to say that I could touch all of those people by 10am each day. I could:

- ➤ speak to immediate family over breakfast and bump into a neighbour by 7am

➤ respond to a group WhatsApp message to family and friends by 7.30am
➤ make a social media post on all platforms about the day ahead by 8am
➤ speak to a client, supplier, team member and students in short Zooms by 10am.

Therefore everyone could have been affected by my mood in some way. That impact could ripple on to their own connections and so on every day; this is Ripple Wave 2. It's a nearly impossible number to predict when you consider this, but even if it was just 10 per person, suddenly that's 100,000 people.

When you think like this, it reminds you of how important it is to control and look after the ripples you create. On a daily basis I could make small positive ripples to 10,000 people, but equally, I could make negative ripples, which doesn't do anyone any favours.

Why don't you have a go at scribbling down some numbers and coming up with an estimate? When I'm in a bad mood, or a little down, I look at my noticeboard in front of me and have a big 10,000 number on it, to remind me to snap out of it and to not make negative ripples but focus my energy on creating positive ones.

There is an argument for some to say that when calculating this maybe you should take out the social media number; that's totally down to you. If I did, it would be 627, but for me social media is a big part of my working world. The point is, whatever the number, we make ripples much further than we might think. Be aware of your number and it will keep you in good stead.

Reflections

As Shakespeare said, 'All the world's a stage, and all the men and women merely players'. I'd add that you're a performer, but you must remember that how you perform makes ripples every day.

Since leaving my previous world to become an entrepreneur, I've learned so much about the ripples I make. I'm more conscious of it than ever but I also don't get too hard on myself if I occasionally have a down day. Despite my best intentions, it will happen, but I do feel more comfort in the fact I know now how important this is and I know it now before my organisation grows further in the years ahead.

For me, it does mean that I now have this mental switch that I just flip automatically in my head as I walk through the office door, about to message someone on my phone or indeed jump on to my first virtual meeting: it turns on an inner message to 'Wake Up, Be There, Make Good Ripples'. It's now just getting built into my DNA and I would encourage you, once you've done the Ripple Number exercise above, to think of the small triggers in your life you can add in which become habits for how you switch yourself on before interacting with people and making your positive daily ripples. I think after only a few days you will begin to notice the benefits.

Takeaways

➤ We all create ripples. Some are big, others are small. Some are positive, others are negative. But we all create ripples.

➤ How these ripples are created is down to you.

➤ Don't be afraid to use your emotions – just do it wisely.

➤ Remember, it's not just what we say but how we say it too – think about your tone of voice and body language when communicating.

➤ Your reach is wider than you realise, but you must nurture your network for it to realise its true potential.

➤ Build your brand – show people why they should trust you.

➤ Make this your mantra: *Wake Up, Be There, Make Good Ripples*.

I hope this level has really introduced you nicely into creating ripples. If you imagine yourself as a pebble being thrown into a pond, it's a good way to visualise the importance of these two words and indeed the importance of your attitude. We will now begin to dive into key areas which can support you in your efforts of making positive ripples on a daily basis.

Level 2

Being Positively Relentless

Being positively relentless is a trait I've spotted in successful people in all walks of life. I actually believe it's a non-negotiable trait required to be successful and create ripples far and wide. You can't be relentless every now and then, and you can't let positivity come and go. If you want to create impactful positive ripples every day that have a profound impact, it's time to make a pledge to yourself to live each day with a relentless but positive attitude.

Being 'positively relentless' is something I first thought of when I began to analyse the traits in those people around me who were successful and happy. I realised it was a combination that was required to be successful very early on. In this level, we're going to look at where positivity comes from, how being relentless can be embraced without running yourself into the ground, and how with simple goal setting we can get started being positively relentless today.

Positive mental attitude

Napoleon Hill first explored the concept of a 'positive mental attitude' in his book *Think and Grow Rich*, published in 1937. He looked at how success in life was linked to having a positive mindset: 'A positive mental attitude is the starting point of all riches, whether they be riches of a material nature or intangible riches.'[8] He explored 14 different concepts, many of which centred around the mind, including 'desire', 'imagination' and 'the brain'. He also put forward the idea that success was due to those in the 'habit' of thinking success – *he was one of the first people to begin linking visualisation to success.* Habit has a huge role to play.

It is a myth, of course, to think that those who think positively never have trials or tribulations in their life, but they've probably got a different attitude to them. Rather than a failure, they might see it as a lesson. Rather than their darkest days, they might see it as an opportunity to bring light. Rather than frustration, it might be their fuel and energy for pushing forwards. *The more you face each problem with a sense of positivity, the more the habit of positivity is embedded and reinforced.*

To me, a positive mental attitude is more than just smiling and looking happy. It is a public display of how you feel, but it's also what you think when you're alone. It's your own thoughts when you remove the social media filter away from your own life and, ultimately, it's seeing the good and the opportunity in a crisis when others only see dismay and ruin. It is *not* about ignoring or avoiding low points; we need to have troughs to appreciate the

---

8 Hill, N. (2004) *Think and Grow Rich*. Vermilion.

peaks.[9] But a person with a positive mindset will be less constrained by the negative phrase 'can't' and instead will see possibilities to solve problems. When a goal is in sight they are then inspired to move to it, reach it and go grab it.

Positive people

We're all capable of harnessing a positive attitude, but some people are better at it than others. We all know people like this and they make great role models. For me, a few spring to mind, one being my first employer.

When I was 13 years old, I was desperate to start earning some money, so one Saturday morning I walked down to the closest business to my house, which happened to be a pub, and knocked on the door. I was greeted by the two beaming smiles of the married couple who were the landlords and owners of the pub. I said, 'Good morning, my name is David and I'm looking for a job.' They smiled, looked down at me and replied, 'You had better come in then, David.'

At that age, there was only one possible job I could do in the pub and that was wash the dishes, and I loved it. I loved being in such a busy but positive enterprise, especially at the weekend. The restaurant was packed, the bar was always full, and the landlords made it such an enjoyable place to work. (Okay, getting to eat the spare chips in the kitchen with some peppercorn sauce after a night shift was delightful!)

However manic it got, however challenging it was in the kitchen when the chef lost their head, the owners would be calm, would be positive and would always have

---

9 http://thinksimplenow.com/happiness/the-5-myths-of-positive-mental-attitude

a smile on their faces. It didn't mean that they would shy away from a difficult conversation or not get serious from time to time, but they realised that if they were positive, the team would be positive and ultimately it would help with their vision for the business and the customer perception of always having a great experience visiting their pub.

Another person I immediately picture when I think of positive people is my coach. I've always believed in the power of coaches, not just on the sports field but also in a professional context. My coach has been with me for nearly a decade now and her positivity always rubs off on me – it's infectious. As a successful entrepreneur, some of this might come from her own successes and experiences, and I know she enjoys sharing in the success of others. But when I speak to her, she listens, sees the opportunities in a situation and helps me through to a conclusion. I especially love that she always finishes off our sessions with power quotes or comments which then make me feel a little stronger or more positive as I bounce to the next challenge!

Some people believe you shouldn't pay for coaching or need to, but I disagree. I realised the value of a professional paid coach in the first few minutes of working with her. After meeting her at a business event, we agreed to meet for a coffee. I think it's fair to say I turned up in an informal dress code (shorts and flip-flops – she's never let me forget this!). I bought her a coffee and then sat down for my coaching session. She looked me up and down and in the back of her head I think she thought this guy isn't serious, so she went tough on me immediately. She asked me to describe my business and what it does. I did. She laughed, stood up and said, 'Your business doesn't or shouldn't be doing that – it can be bigger. You need to think bigger. I'll see you in three weeks' time and you'll have a much better answer to that question.' She literally left her coffee and went.

My immediate reaction was, 'Blimey – she's rude', but within minutes of my coaching session, where I found myself alone with two coffees now, I realised what she meant and for the next three weeks my head was spinning on that particular question again. When we eventually sat down again (and this time I was a little more cautious about whether or not I should actually get her a coffee!), she asked me the same question. I nailed it and she said, 'Now we can work together. You've proven you care; you can think and, importantly, you can think big.' The rest was history, but her positivity throughout is something I've always noticed.

The last positive person I want to highlight is another former boss because he had a huge impact on me and still does. He was amazingly positive, despite the heat and pressures of working in a professional sales role in a corporate tech giant. He was a South African businessman, larger than life, a great sportsman, but also just an amazing people manager. He knew it was his job to grow and nurture talent, despite the day-to-day challenges of living a sales life. There is one specific moment I remember in particular where he left me feeling like a ten-foot giant – even after I had lost a multi-million pound deal at the end of a financial year!

Rather than beat me up, he sat me down immediately at 5 pm on a Friday to review what had happened, rather than letting me stew on it over the weekend. Having gone through it together, we came to the logical conclusion that there was next to nothing I could have done differently (there was an accounting error on the part of our customer that no one was aware of until it was too late). This wasn't a case of 'false growth mindset', which I'll come to shortly, but was the logical truth. He then finished the meeting and said, 'Now, get out of my office. You're awesome at what you do – go have a beer on me.' He turned me from feeling negative to positive – even optimistic about the next financial quarter – within a 30-minute conversation. To this day, he remains a close friend and, despite us not working together now, he still has this remarkably positive impact on my attitude and approach to life. (It sounds like a simple thing, but I also realised how powerful a conversation on the last working day of the week can be to help an employee bounce into work the following week. So I make a big effort to say thank you where I can on this day, and let one of my team know how special they are to our business.)

Developing a growth mindset

I have no doubt you will have people in your mind who breed positivity in your life too. But are these people born with this strong sense of positivity or is it developed over time?

The American psychologist Carol Dweck coined the term 'growth mindset', meaning that talents and abilities aren't fixed and they can be developed – I agree with this. You can improve and 'cultivate' your efforts to be better. Her research began 30 years ago, focusing on resilience in students when it came to attitudes about failure – some were able to take it on the chin as it were, and some were devastated by it. Dweck's research brought her to the conclusion that there are 'underlying beliefs people have about learning and intelligence. When students believe they can get smarter, they understand that effort makes them stronger. Therefore they put in extra time and effort, and that leads to higher achievement.'[10]

Science confirms it really is possible to stretch our brains! Brain plasticity, as it is known, has shown that existing neurons can be strengthened and new ones can be connected. We do this by adopting good habits from our diet, sleep and exercise, asking questions and being strategic thinkers. To know that we have this much power over enhancing our brains demonstrates how the relentless drive can have positive impacts. We can really develop ourselves to be better and in a positive way.

But if not reinforced properly, there is a danger of negativity to this – a 'false growth mindset'. This is the belief that a teacher or a coach could foster a growth mindset merely by telling students they are doing well even if there is no effort or it's not the case. This is often done out of fear of hurting or upsetting an individual. However, surely it's better to be honest and reflective with our encouragement, rather than telling someone that they've done something great when they really haven't?

A personal example of a false mindset I developed was when I was at university. I remember being told I was an excellent public speaker, despite having very little training. I did enjoy being on my feet and was passionate about the subject I was studying, so speaking about those topics in public came easily to me. The problem was that speaking was in a more informal environment and the praise was from friends and family, not actually from those who spoke publicly or in a corporate environment themselves. When I was asked to present out of the blue on the first day of my new job out of university, I went into it with an

---

10 www.mindsetworks.com/science

unfounded sense of confidence – and failed dismally. I did have an element of natural structure when I spoke (I always knew every speech needed a start, middle and end), but I was seriously underprepared in this instance, whereas in the past it came naturally because I was so familiar with the topics being presented. The 'friendly' praise that I had had in the past hadn't really been constructive, although nice at the time, and had meant I put myself on a pedestal that I didn't deserve to be on. Praise when it is not really deserved diminishes the overall outcome because it does not address the areas that a student or indeed an employee needs to improve on.

Since that day, I vowed never to be that bad again and have dedicated a huge amount of time to working on the art of public speaking and making sure I'm fully prepared ahead of any speaking event. The biggest ways I sped up this learning and personal development were:

➤ listening to podcasts of great speakers and spotting patterns

➤ creating a 'presentation' one-pager to help me prepare for every opportunity I ever had – this allowed me to control what I could control and reflect and improve

➤ building in serious preparation and rehearsal opportunities before getting on stage.

These small tweaks allowed me to build up my confidence, style and approach on stage to now allow me to be an accomplished speaker, but I will never take it for granted and will seek to continue to improve to be the best I possibly can be.

It's happened since in other situations but actually

in reverse – I was beginning to deliver poor feedback. I found myself falling into this trap on a few occasions, of encouraging a false growth mindset as I moved from being an entrepreneur to a business owner who employed people. In the early days I was still developing as a leader and as a manager of people (and I still am). Despite my business developing, managing people on a daily basis was actually a new challenge for me, which I approached with little thought at the beginning, regrettably – I just assumed I would be good at it!

At the start, I didn't want negativity in the small team and wanted to encourage positivity, but I wasn't using the growth mindset theory in the appropriate way. I was giving praise when it wasn't really deserved and it didn't help the business or that individual. The work from some people was sometimes just 'adequate'. There was nothing too great or too wrong about it and I would find myself saying 'thank you', rather than giving direction and guidance on what I expected from that person. *The feedback loop is key if indeed you want to build a world-class organisation*, which was my aspiration. But I was missing a key cog in achieving that, and that's coaching people appropriately. Now I know how unhelpful that style was; one of the pillars of our organisation is 'excellence' – when you have this as a pillar it makes it easier to direct people back to it, even before they show you their work or ask for feedback.

Even more recently, we nearly fell back into the trap of the business of doing this but on a wider scale. In our internal messaging group we had a section called 'pats', and within my communication meetings a time for 'public pats', for people to share 'pats on the back' publicly to another employee on the messaging section or in a meeting – the idea was to help drive recognition.

Although this was launched with good intentions, one of my team spoke up at a meeting and said, 'I hate pats – we're patting people for doing their job and we shouldn't be doing that.' He had a point! This wasn't about people doing work at an average level anymore as we had moved on from that as a team and the level of work was much higher now. But we weren't improving because we were basically saying well done for doing your job. What this person felt was that we needed to be more specific and use 'pats' for when people really go above and beyond. We shouldn't normalise the day job as good enough and, if we didn't change our approach to it, it wouldn't necessarily be a false mindset but it also wouldn't be a growth mindset approach – it basically wasn't achieving anything. Following him raising this issue, the channel became much quieter and sometimes no public pats were given on a team meeting, but when it did happen, the individual and the team really recognised it because it meant much more than the pats of the past.

Find your motivation

When we look at positivity and how that is cultivated, one of the key things that needs to be established is *motivation*. The desire to do well and improve even by the smallest amount needs to be recognised before the positive gains can be fully realised.

The psychologist Abraham Maslow looked at motivation and put it in a pyramid as a hierarchy of needs. It is based around the principles of humans having basic needs that must be satisfied (physiological ones, such as food and water at the bottom of the pyramid, then safety, belonging and esteem) before they are able to reach the top of the pyramid – the needs for growth and achieving one's full potential (see image below). Some people point to this theory to show why those from privileged backgrounds have more likelihood of gaining success because they will have had all their basic needs met and so can progress to growth and eventual success.[11] But we also know, however, that those who are disadvantaged and perhaps lacking in those basic needs can flip this theory and be equally destined for great things too, despite the obstacles they may face. They can be more driven because of these challenges. Whatever a person's starting point, a growth mindset is an important tool, which entails leading from the front in order to be useful and so everyone can benefit.

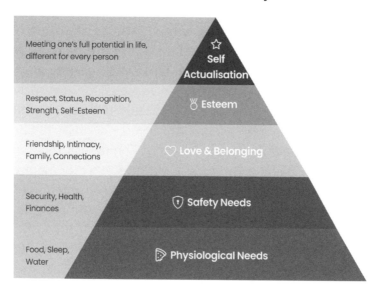

In a similar vein to Maslow's hierarchy of needs, Martin Seligman, another American psychologist, found seven habits of happy people (and as we know,

---

11 www.simplypsychology.org/maslow.html

happiness can be part of our positive behaviour and bring positive outcomes). One of these habits is having a positive mindset, and he explores the use of optimism in particular. Those who are optimistic, Seligman suggests, are able to see opportunity within any situation, even the most difficult ones. (He also looks at other aspects of happiness such as following a healthy lifestyle and being kind – areas that we will come back to.)[12]

But we also need to remember that 'toxic positivity' exists. What do I mean by this? Just in the same way the growth mindset theory can be misused, positivity can be misunderstood and deemed to be a cure to all problems. Some positivity undermines itself by not addressing where there might be issues or an individual isn't facing problems head on. There is often an assumption that if you are not continuing to be positive during times of stress, it means you're inadequate or weak in some way.[13] This can be especially true when we consider how social media is used to show only the best side of life and people strive to emulate it.

I've worked with people where sometimes this has been a problem. It is typically with the 'joker' or 'happy-go-lucky' person who uses positivity as their main asset in a team. The problem is when this blurs into their day job and they forget that it's not all about positivity, but delivering too. On some occasions, nice people have used positivity to their advantage, not necessarily deliberately but in a way that doesn't actually help them. You need to have a good balance, but not use a positive mindset to plaster over cracks.

---

12 www.pursuit-of-happiness.org/science-of-happiness/
13 www.healthline.com/health/mental-health/toxic-positivity-during-the-pandemic#What-is-toxic-positivity?

Harness positivity

Feelings of doubt or uncertainty aren't uncommon in stressful times but, in such situations, we can harness the power of positivity to open up the mind to more possibilities. But where do we begin? The fact that just by looking at something positively can have that impact means that we need very little to get the immediate benefits of this powerful emotion; it doesn't require any monetary input or great upheaval. Many people look to their immediate surroundings and find joy in nature, for example, to have an uplift in their mood, or visit their favourite place to get an instant boost, or go for a walk to get beneficial fresh air or sunlight. The sun can have a dramatic impact on people's moods and it's why vitamin D is so important (I do also take daily tablets to help!).

Our working surroundings are key. I'm fortunate to have an office five minutes from my house. It's a studio office located not too far from our main premises. It's perfect for me to separate work from home and have a place to do the confidential work I need to do when running a business. However, the first office I had in the building didn't have a window. I wasn't fussed at the time as I was desperate to get something. However, over time I realised that no natural light was having such an impact on me, so when an office came up with a window, it dramatically changed everything for me for the good. It really was beginning to damage my mental health after six months.

I've also read up on the importance of plants around you when you work. It's predicted to help improve morale and productivity by up to 15 per cent.[14] These small

---

14 www.theguardian.com/money/2014/aug/31/plants-offices-workers-productive-minimalist-employees

things can have the biggest impact and they can set you on the path to achieving greater things. This goes hand in hand with the positive mindset and forms part of how we harness this power.

As we have seen, there really are many ways in which we can develop our own sources of inspiration, which in turn helps us to think about being positive and then channelling this to make positive thoughts.

For me, my positivity comes from the fact my work is linked to my passions, and I try to control negativity – not run away from it! For example, I've found that the most significant way my positivity can be 'dented' is through what so many of us have come to rely on – my phone! I might read something on social media which I disagree with or think is unfair. This would impact my positivity, so an easy fix was limiting the people I follow (and removing 'negative eggs' as I like to call them) and simply reducing my time on social media.

The second thing that was affecting my positivity, and still related to my phone, was my emails. With more of our work being virtual now, I found myself exposed to emails more than ever. But emails have the power to take you out of one 'room' into a completely different one in a second. And emails can make you feel a whole mix of emotions: positivity, frustration and negativity. An email read at 9.30 pm or 7 am would make no difference to the outcome, but it could take me away from my family or could potentially affect my mood before sleep and affect the pattern of my sleep – so why read it? I therefore deleted my email app from my phone and it not only improved my levels of positivity, it also didn't affect the quality of my work.

To be clear, this isn't me escaping my inbox – I'm just looking at it at a time when I can actually deal with it. Reading emails at the wrong time can change your mood before bed, around friends and indeed your family. I remember once reading an email before helping to put the children down to sleep and found myself reading my four-year-old son his favourite bedtime story. However, I was on autopilot: I was reading the words and thinking about work. I was appalled at myself that I couldn't even just focus for a few minutes at that time to make the story as fun as possible and I knew it was down to the way I was dealing with my emails – hence the change, and I don't regret it at all.

Without a shadow of a doubt, positivity is a good thing for our mentality – at the end of the day, what's the alternative – a negative attitude? What will that achieve? Much better is a pragmatic one, ready to deal with life's challenges.

Of course, positive thinking on its own doesn't extract the results – it's the action that accompanies it. Entrepreneurs, leaders and individuals don't get success just by thinking positively. The 'thought' is the first step and then comes the 'doing'.

Being relentless

To be fully rounded in the positivity stakes, there also needs to be an element of *relentlessness*, focus and drive. An important factor for any entrepreneur, leader or go-getter is learning how to manage the inevitable trials and errors that come with success. It is the relentless drive that carries a person through those hard times and the belief that they will make it to the other side with the help of a 'positive mental attitude'.

If you hear any Manchester United player who played under Sir Alex Ferguson in their glory years speak, the common word from all of them is 'relentless'. It was a brutal environment: unless you were up to the mark in your commitment, you didn't belong. Sir Alex knew what was required to succeed and a relentless drive was critical, along with that positive attitude. This led him to winning 38 trophies over 26 years – quite an extraordinary feat.

One person in that team who embodied this, and still does to this day, is Cristiano Ronaldo. As a football fan I knew he was committed, but it was fully clear to me only when I heard Phil Neville, a former player and former manager, say that on the first day in charge of the national women's team, all he did was put up Ronaldo's daily routine on the wall. He explained that Ronaldo spent less than ten per cent of his time being coached and his success was down to his relentlessness and commitment to his goals. Here is an example of a typical day in the life of Ronaldo:

- ➤ 6 am: Train
- ➤ 8 am: Nap for 90 mins
- ➤ 9:30 am: Breakfast ham and cheese, yoghurt and fruit juice
- ➤ 10:30 am: Work out
- ➤ 12:30 am: Nap
- ➤ 2:00 pm Lunch of chicken and salad
- ➤ 3:00 pm: Nap
- ➤ 4:30 pm: Lunch #2 of tuna with salad, eggs and olives
- ➤ 7 pm: Dinner of meat or fish
- ➤ 8 pm: Time with family and friends
- ➤ 10 pm: Swim session
- ➤ 11 pm: Relax and go to bed

You can see why he has won 'World Player of the Year' five times. *The ability to maintain positivity and stay focused is the driving force to being relentless.*

But is there a correlation between relentlessness and time committed to a goal? Is it as simple as that? In his book *Outliers: The Story of Success*, Malcolm Gladwell suggests that 10,000 hours of practice will make you an expert in something. But it's more than just the number, it's about the 'deliberate' practice. You can use this theory to decide if you are putting in enough *deliberate* practice in your area of expertise. Are you *consciously* practising? Are you consolidating what you have learned?

The words 'conscious' and 'consolidate' are important in determining whether your mind is actively seeking to improve in whatever it is you are trying to be better at. Going through the motions may allow some information to permeate through to your subconscious, but it won't have the same impact as being 'mindful' during the process. A lack of that mindfulness is why occasionally you see child sports stars with pushy parents who end up not making it – mainly because those parents have pushed them into a sport, relentlessly committed them to it, but in their heart of hearts the child never wanted to do it or do it to that level. Hence they just go through the motions, despite the hours committed, never being fully in the moment.

Avoiding burnout

The idea of being relentless – the expectation to always be on or in a work state of mind – can seem unappealing and even exhausting to some people. It has connotations of people who can't relax or even have unreasonably high expectations of those around them. Leaders who are relentless may be high achievers, but does this come at a cost?

There are anecdotal examples everywhere of high achievers who have suffered at the hands of success.

They have lost friends and family because of jealousy, expectations that they pay for everything when socialising, being targeted for handouts from individuals who need medical treatment, feeling vulnerable because of the high monetary value of their possessions, or being targeted for fraud and extortion if the monetary gain has come from success. Sometimes, not money but status comes from it, or even fame can be a by-product. These shouldn't put you off success, but they are things that people should be aware of and need to learn how to prepare for them.

From both a psychological and physiological perspective, there is a danger that you can experience burnout or lose sight of the simple things, like a Tantalean punishment, having all the good things, but not being able to enjoy them, having a feeling of disconnect. (Tantalus is a figure from Greek mythology who was the rich but wicked king of Sipylus. For attempting to serve his own son at a feast with the gods, he was punished by Zeus to forever go thirsty and hungry in Hades despite being made to stand in a pool of water and almost within reach of a fruit tree.) Recent research shows that 60 per cent of SME owners work more than 50 hours a week and take less than three weeks' holiday a year. On the face of it, running a business can look extremely appealing and much of it is, but it will always be extremely hard to escape the fact it is a 24/7 responsibility.

For me, I realised how much I needed to have 'burnout' under control in the first year of trying to really get the business going. I was actually experiencing chest pains – something which is quite scary when you're a young man. I was out walking the dog with my wife and said that I needed to stop. I was really struggling with my breathing and went immediately to the doctor. Luckily, these pains were coming from a period of stress and it was a case of getting the balance back in my life (as well as cutting out caffeine). I was doing and having to deal with too much and my body was beginning to say no. I was starting the business, still doing a full-time job, trying to buy a house, getting ready for a wedding and then, to top it off, my wife had a major cancer scare that needed treatment. There were an abnormal number of things going on and after having these pains, I realised I couldn't push myself that hard again; otherwise it wouldn't just be a big burnout period but could actually have an everlasting impact on my health. I created a list of everything that I was worried about or involved in. With my family, I worked on what I could take off the worry list and I began to say no to things to just reduce the burden on my shoulders – It was a defining point in my life.

I have to say, the manager I had at the time within my full-time job also realised things were a little too much for me and said something that I would never forget. He could tell in my weekly review something wasn't quite adding up, so dropped everything, got on the train to come and see me, sat me down and said, 'David, I've only got one thing to say to you: the sun will come out tomorrow. You've got so many things going on in your life, and some of these worries you don't need to have and you certainly don't need to multiply them in your head (he was referring to my full-time job with him). Even if we don't hit the sales numbers, the sun will come up tomorrow and new opportunities will shine.' His man-management of me that day was spot on and helped release some of the pressure and worries that I had created in my head.

In this scenario I was getting burnout because I had too much going on, but even when you get tunnelled focus on what your priority is, I still believe and know that relentlessness and drive is required to achieve your goals; success doesn't just happen.

Gut feeling

There is a danger though that the constant drive means there is a risk of error and not listening to gut feelings of concern. Being 'worried' is associated with caring, but that's not to say relentless people don't care; in fact, they may care very much – but mistakes can happen. It's easy to show poor judgement and not prioritise your time effectively. It means you can end up fire-fighting all the time rather than putting value in your business where it is needed most. People can lose sight of what is happening and failure is waiting around the corner.

However, relentlessness, or a period of your life where you're relentless, is required when hitting certain goals. As long as you *control your relentlessness* and do not let it become out of control, I maintain it's a good thing. I would encourage people not to fall into the camp of 'That's all well and good, David – I don't want to become like those people', because my answer is that you don't need to. Don't use *those people*'s errors and mistakes as an excuse for not committing yourself to something – learn from them.

Being relentless doesn't have to mean spending hours in the office. It can be immersing yourself in a podcast instead of music. To call someone in the car to ask their opinion on something. To think about something focused when you run or walk. Ask a friend for their thoughts when in a pub. It's actually the contagious energy you have, your passion, which makes you positively relentless.

In my case it's the energy I've had since the idea for my first business – anyone who's been around me over the years will vouch for this, particularly at the start when I would literally talk to anyone about it. When I was actually trying to do private crowdfunding, I would walk around with the pitch in a nice little black booklet and ask if people wanted to hear what I was about to start. People would laugh for a second, then I would get started and then I could see their interest start to be piqued. I learned something after every elevator pitch – I had different reactions, different questions and feedback. Some agreed to invest, others didn't. But the positivity and relentlessness helped. Eventually, when we landed our first substantial angel investor, I asked him why he wanted to invest and he said the three Ps: passion, personality and passion again. I think this was coming across from my positively relentless attitude to our new venture!

My message: get relentless but get focused too.

Bringing it all together

Let's remind ourselves of the positives of 'being positively relentless'. It means:

➤ you are in control of how you want to feel
➤ you acknowledge how you react to a challenge
➤ you see clarity and opportunity in a crisis
➤ you're focused on achieving your goals and making an impact
➤ you don't question your commitment to your work.

So where do I start in embracing this to create the ripples I want to create?

Top tip: Goal setting: The Christmas CV

You can't be relentless without knowing what goals you want to hit.

Pablo Picasso said this of setting goals: 'Our goals can only be reached through a vehicle of a plan, in which we must fervently believe, and upon which we must vigorously act. There is no other route to success.'[15] Goals have to be made on a conscious level and it's this consciousness that affects action; we have to decide what is beneficial to our wellbeing and set goals to achieve it.

For me, what I began to do is set my goals by writing my future 'Christmas CV'. Every year in the downtime between Christmas and New Year, I would rewrite my CV and update my LinkedIn profile, even though I had no motivation to leave my job. I would then rewrite it how I wanted it to look in a year's time and literally date it one year later. I would grab a highlighter and mark the things on that CV which I had actually not yet achieved. Then it was simple: that was my goal for the next year. Whether it meant that I was going to close £10 million pounds of business, get my promotion at work, raise £3,000 for charity or go and win a cricket league, it didn't matter. My CV was always covering my work, but also my hobbies and charity commitments and the goals I would set for myself within those, meaning I would have a balanced approach to my goal setting and not just all work, work, work.

---

15 https://positivepsychology.com/goal-setting

I still do it to this day (albeit with my LinkedIn Profile, rather than my CV), even as an entrepreneur, as it continues to keep me focused, not only for the long term, but also the short term in the year ahead. I believe it's why I continue to feel relentless, but also why I continue to believe I've got more energy today than at any other point in my career *and I feel like I'm saying that as every year goes by!* This will help you focus and become relentless over time too. The positivity will come if you have a balanced set of goals on your Christmas CV which are linked to your inner passions.

Here's a glimpse of one of my Christmas CVs:

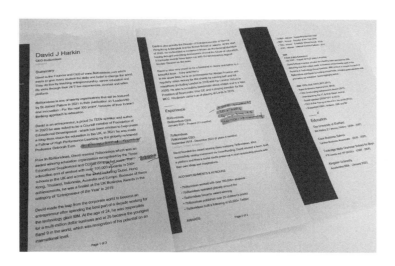

Reflections

Whatever your pathway in life, you have no choice but to be positively relentless if you want to be successful in what you do. By being positive, you will be that person who spots opportunities when no one else does. You will be that person who will want to go and grab them, and you will be that person who will be relentless when you face the inevitable hurdles that come your way.

The relentlessness needs to be managed, but don't be fearful of it; embrace it, control it and utilise it. Sometimes it might be a period of days, weeks, months or years when you need to give 200 per cent commitment to something, but at least at the end of it, no matter the results, you will have no regrets – you will not look back and wish that you did more because you know in your heart of hearts you did everything you could.

As you begin to reflect on this level, think about when being positive in your life has proven to be an asset to not only you as an individual, but also when you've been in a team, whether or not you lead it. What made you positive? What impact did it have on you and others?

Have a go at your Christmas CV and see if it gives you that little bit more of a focus in the months ahead. Don't forget what Napoleon Hill says about habits. The more this mindset is practised, the more it can happen and you create that positive cycle. *Let's get positive. Let's get relentless*.

Takeaways

➤ Develop a growth mindset – celebrate success but also learn from mistakes and failures.
➤ Practice a growth mindset – it soon develops a positive cycle.
➤ Increase your positivity and drive by finding what motivates you.
➤ Maintaining positivity and focus is the driving force to being relentless and goal-setting is the only way.
➤ *Let's get positive. Let's get relentless.*

Now that we've revisited the importance of positivity and relentlessness combined, it's time to consider if being busy is a good thing or if there is an alternative. On to Level 3...

Level 3

Being Brilliantly Busy

The words we speak reinforce our mentality. They can indirectly or accidentally create perceptions of situations which sometimes simply aren't true. One of these words is busy. A lot of people moan about being busy. Some people are busy for busy's sake; some are busybodies. Successful people, people who enjoy what they do, however, don't seem to complain about being busy. Those that are committed to making positive ripples don't see themselves as being busy – they see themselves as being brilliantly busy!

It's time to stop being busy and become brilliantly busy. It's always been a frustration of mine when people use the word busy in such a negative way. In this level we will explore its origins, why it's used, how busyness is perceived around the world and, by the end of the level, we will move to reflecting hard on how you're spending your time to maximise your ripples. Let's move on with Level 3...

Busyness

The word 'busy' has a few meanings, being used to describe disparate or uncoordinated patterns or colours ('that rug is too busy for this room'); or when a telephone line is engaged and therefore 'busy'; or if there are too many people in one place; and even to describe someone as officious or meddlesome (a busybody). It can, and does, often offer us a negative view of life.

But there are times when it doesn't; for example, times when you have longed to be busy, especially if that is in terms of gaining more revenue and sales but have had little response to your offerings. To then find yourself busy can in fact be a huge positive and you can feel productive. But even then, as you get busier, it's likely the negative connotations start to surface. 'The grass is always greener on the other side' – it's a well-used phrase. How often we wish for a hot summer and then we get it 'it's too hot for my liking'. Being busy falls into a similar category – suddenly being busy means you are no longer able to do the things you want and life has taken over.

'Busy' can also become a byword for wanting to get out of doing something; for example, avoiding a discussion with someone who takes time out of your busy day, or telling your children you can't possibly play another game as you are too busy. In his book *The Big Leap*, Gay Hendricks agrees that it is an avoidance tactic. If there was an emergency, then you would find yourself able to give that time, so it's not about time at all but how you are perceiving and prioritising time. Maybe being busy is all about time management. It also depends on your feelings about what you're doing when you're busy. If you enjoy what you do, being busy is positive and it's 'good' busy. If you don't enjoy what you do, you might feel drained and unable to juggle it all – then it's 'bad' busy.

Work smarter

I find that there is a blurry line between being busy and being *productive*, but there is nonetheless a difference between them. Being busy is about working harder, while *being productive is about working smarter*. Being busy is frantic, while *being productive is focused*.

We've all heard the phrase 'Work smarter, not harder'. It was first used by the industrial engineer Allen F. Morgenstern in the 1930s. He had created a simplification programme to enable people to produce more without increasing effort. It's now synonymous with better work practices and finding the balance between not only being busy but being able to achieve what you set out to do each day. (Although there also has to be some degree of flexibility and not feeling like a failure if that to-do list hasn't been achieved.)

With the dramatic change in the way that we now work in recent years, with more people working at home, judging how productive, or indeed busy, we are compared to our peers is now extremely hard. Personally, I find myself in two identities on a typical day, the first being 'Virtual Dave', speaking to my clients, team and suppliers in back-to-back virtual meetings. The virtual element no doubt allows me to achieve more than I would ever do otherwise. With travel time significantly reduced, I found this being replaced by more meetings. Whereas in the past, I might be lucky to have two constructive meetings with a client a day (one in the morning and one in the afternoon, with travelling in between), I now find I can do that by 9 am online. I've often said recently that I believe I now do a month's work in a week, compared to what I did in a less remote working world, due to this explosion of online meetings.

I also find that with the travelling reduced, these meetings have shortened in length to get to the point much quicker. Traditionally a meeting would naturally be booked in for one hour and within these meetings, rapport would be built and often conversation would flow even longer about unrelated work issues. Now in a virtual world, where it's harder sometimes to do this, I've found meeting lengths have shortened and are much more concise. This is something of a double-edged sword. On one hand, it's great because you can drive an agenda through quicker, but on the other hand, it's still important to find ways to build great rapport with your clients – this is key to developing successful relationships that will last for many years.

Alongside 'Virtual Dave' is 'Alone Dave', which is me when the Zooms stop. I'm alone and it's back down to me to get focused. I used to desire this, but now I miss the welcome distraction of a hustling, bustling office with sometimes unrelated chats which also indirectly kept me focused on my goals and targets. (Another example of the grass not always being greener on the other side!)

What are you doing with your time?

Being busy, though, is surely what people expect of us, isn't it? It's what we expect of ourselves. If you aren't busy then what are you doing with your time?

It used to be that what people did in their spare time,

or more accurately how much spare time they had, was a measure of their wealth and success. The wealthier and more successful you were, the more time you had off. And spare time still seems to be a measure but now it's more likely *being busy* is synonymous with wealth and success – it suggests someone is in great demand.

Elbert Hubbard, an American writer and publisher (among many other professions) born in the 1850s, once said, 'If you want work well done, select a busy man – the other kind has no time.' From experience, this can be especially irritating for people who are perceived as busy and get more work given to them! I remember my old headteacher once said it to me and I quickly found myself responsible for things I had no interest in doing but did them because I liked that I was considered a person who got things done!

Attitudes towards busyness and how it is perceived can vary across cultures too. In an interview in an *Atlantic* article, researcher Silvia Bellezza discussed what she had found on both sides of the Atlantic in her work.[16] When Americans were shown a lifestyle of someone having a lot of leisure time, the explanation was that the person must not be working, whereas the Mediterranean countries like Greece, Italy and Spain thought there must be an element of wealth that the person can afford all this leisure time. Conversely though, in Silicon Valley it's not deemed 'cool' to discuss your constant busyness and, instead, there seems to be more respect if people know you have been hiking or enjoying some other such activity. It's as much a matter of perception of the word busy as it is an actual concept.

---

16 www.theatlantic.com/business/archive/2017/03/busyness-status-symbol/518178

There's also a generation factor to bring into this. The way we use our time today is vastly different from that of people even ten years ago. Our forebears spent much of their time in stereotypical roles, with women raising large families and doing all the housework, and men working all hours. Now the generations have become more splintered. Generation Z (the ones after the Millennials) were born in an age where technology was on the cusp of huge change. The 90s and early 2000s were a time of huge promise with the dawn of the millennium and mobile phones taking the world by storm. And think of the new generations being born from now: they'll never know what a video player or a CD player was, and they haven't even realised there were once only four TV channels to choose from! (And of course we love to remind them, just like our parents did with us and their parents before them.)

Busyness burnout

In all seriousness, things change and how we perceive busyness can have real and serious consequences. Generation Z typically spend more than six hours on their mobile devices every day, of which three hours a day is on social media. So we can see a picture building up here – the younger generations are busy socialising online and making connections that way. They also have the worst work/life balance. They worry the most out of all the generations about taking time off and how they will be perceived. Some stats that might surprise you:[17]

---

17 www.businessinsider.com/study-gen-z-worst-work-life-balance-2019-11?r=US&IR=T

➤ Nearly a quarter (24 per cent) of Gen Z say they feel guilty taking any time off work, which means they don't take all their paid time off in a year. (They're followed by Millennials, at 19 per cent, Gen Xers at 16 per cent, and Boomers, at eight per cent.)

➤ Another quarter (24 per cent) of Gen Z say they fret that taking all of their allotted vacation time would cause people to judge them at work — and they worry about this much more than any other generation at work. The closest behind them are Millennials, at 15 per cent.

➤ And if Gen Zers *do* go on vacation, they are the most likely to say they feel under pressure to check email or voicemail while they're on holiday (47 per cent), followed by Millennials (40 per cent).

This will cause extreme burnout and sets a precedent for their working life. Other generations have tried to find a way to avoid these pitfalls, but perhaps we have all felt like this at some point in our lives, so maybe some see it as a rite of passage in becoming an adult, whereas others would rather none of us ever have to feel like that. Perhaps we should be kinder to different generations, instead of constantly reminding them that 'You don't know what it was like when I was young' and reeling off all your hard times as a way to demonstrate that it's a normal way of life. Remember, we used to send children up chimneys, but someone realised that was a bad idea! Maybe we should begin trying to strike a balance that is fairer to *everyone* regardless of age.

I think I became very aware of this on one of our courses we did with students where we would actually take them into a business for three days and create a real-life working environment for them, asking them to respond to a tender. Thirty students would walk into offices of a multinational company, whose job it was to host them and then launch a tender to the students. My team would then work with the students, turn them into newbie consultants and over three days prepare them to submit the tenders and pitch their ideas to a board of directors. This was an amazing educational and work experience opportunity combined. However, what was really interesting is what the multinational companies asked the students for. The tender they wanted a response to was always, 'How do we attract and retain Generation Z talent?' This was what the first company we ever worked with asked and then they all wanted to know the answers to this. It produced some fascinating responses from students who were in that generation about what they expected from a workplace. However, it was sharing the research and seeing the dramatic shift in opinions to those even I held (I'm maybe 10–15 years older than them) which made me conscious of how different generations are and how we all need to be aware of one another. For example, over 75 per cent of Generation Z students wanted a daily check-in with their boss. To me this sounded like micromanagement and a nightmare, but when they explained that they're from a generation of 'instant notification', then it makes sense. Speaking to your management once a week is the polar opposite of getting 50 likes on an Instagram post.

Busier than ever

So are we busier now than we have ever been? A number of academic studies suggest that *we're not as busy as we think* and time spent in work hasn't increased since the 1960s. What has changed is our attitudes towards being busy, with many people seeing it as a badge of honour.[18]

Despite how life has changed over time, and despite how different cultures around the world use time in different ways, the one thing that has always fascinated me is that time seems to be the biggest problem in every industry, business, government or organisation around the world. But time, not money or oil, is the only common currency which is consistent across all of the planet's population. No matter where you are in the world, there are 525,600 minutes each year and it's down to each and every one of us how we utilise that time.

I think my fascination with time came from an early conversation with a senior person at work. I asked him how he went about hitting his targets and were there any keys to his success. He said to me it was all about valuing time because there were only 252 days a year to sell (excluding taking holidays!). 52*5 equals 260 and, if you remove national holidays, it would leave you with 252. He therefore believed that every day was valuable and that you shouldn't and couldn't let time drift. One working week was two per cent of your time over a year to hit your target. He encouraged me to think about how I could carve this time up and think about 'opportunity cost' – which effectively means if I was doing X, I wouldn't be doing Y – so make sure whatever X was, it was a good

---

18 https://theconversation.com/obsessed-with-being-busy-a-historical-perspective-may-help-you-out-107755

use of my time. This was a fascinating thought to leave with a young, hungry professional and to this day I'm constantly analysing what I'm doing with my time. I've even built my own utilisation reports which work out on any given week what percentage of the time is on emails, in meetings, strategically thinking, resting, etc. This allows me to analyse myself in ways many don't but, importantly, to make sure I'm utilising every week as best I can. My goal at the moment is to up my 'thinking time' as much as possible because I'm finding it incredibly difficult to create clear space to make some awesome decisions. I want to be brilliantly busy but also brilliantly doing stuff which makes a massive impact.

Perhaps, therefore, it is a lexical change rather than a physical change which might explain our constant need to use the word. *There is an element of choice in how busy we are.* For example, think about the time we spend on our devices. According to the RescueTime app, we spend between three hours 15 mins and four and a half hours a day on our phones! That's up to one-sixth of your day. For some people the mobile phone has become their everything – text messenger, email system, social media, news outlet, online shopping, gaming. You can even watch TV and listen to the radio. So perhaps it's not the 'what' in this case but the 'how'.

Time for a change

Don't get me wrong; there will be times in our lives when we've got a lot to do, but saying 'I'm busy' when asked 'How are you?' is actually the grown-up version of saying 'Sorry, my dog ate my homework'. I wonder if it's an excuse that adults use regularly to hide their real, deep inner feelings related to their happiness? Might be, might not be. And while we are here, let's think about those idioms and sayings that are so popular in the English language. Here are some that maybe you say, some positive and some negative:

➤ *snowed under*
➤ *bite off more than you can chew*
➤ *finger in every pie*
➤ *go the extra mile*
➤ *no pain, no gain*
➤ *time flies when you're having fun.*

It's a good exercise in observing our own language – not just when we say the word busy, but using these and many other idioms. Are they meaningful? What impression do they give? Perhaps this is a good time to explore your language use and find some new expressions. Those who repeatedly use the word 'busy' are maybe using it as a comfort blanket without even knowing why they've not explored all of their passions.

There are also the psychological aspects of the word 'busy' that can have a powerful effect. An article in the *Washington Post* lists various reasons why it can be detrimental to us, for example stopping us from being 'present' and risking losing the enjoyment of the moment. The word itself can add stress to life and cause disconnection. Surely how busy you are is a choice? When people complain of being busy it can cause resentment. If you are truly unhappy with how busy you are, then maybe it's time to make a change. This can come from discussing your work commitments with your boss or it could mean a whole career change. How you choose to be busy is up to you. Be honest with people if you can't be with them, especially your loved ones. Rather than saying you're busy, tell them that you're tired and want a good night's sleep, or you have other plans but would love to see them another time. Just don't always fall back on, 'I'm busy'.[19]

Leaders and managers must also be so careful in the use of this keyword. Constantly telling people that you're either busy, or giving the impression that you don't have any time for staff, can have so many negative impacts. One will be on how innovative and fearless the team are in sharing ideas with you. The mindset is quick to set within the ranks that if you're too busy, then 'why would he or she want to hear my little idea?'. This can be beyond damaging as you have no idea what that idea could be, and no doubt the idea has been generated because that employee can see an improvement. That is something you would surely like to hear as all improvement brings benefits. Suggestions like this can be linked to any of five benefits:

1. productivity gains
2. employee wellbeing
3. client satisfaction
4. cost saving
5. revenue generation.

In my experience, literally every idea in an organisation can be linked to one of these and through your use of the word 'busy' or perceived busyness, you're directly squashing innovation and potentially missing out on

19 www.washingtonpost.com/news/inspired-life/wp/
2015/03/17/six-reasons-why-you-shouldnt-use-the-b-word-so-much

millions of ideas on an annual basis.

The ability to be honest rather than just resorting to the 'b' word may help to maintain those relationships. There are those who suggest we should stop using the word completely and it would make us happier. The constant use of it can cause a disconnect between people as we lose sight of what it is that others need from us – we are too quick to say we are busy. These disconnects can have negative ripple effects for others and indeed those who need help or feel like they are a burden because they are scared to disturb their busy friends and family.

The art of being idle

Cognitive scientist Andrew Smart advocates in his book *Autopilot: The Art and Science of Doing Nothing* that we should try and do nothing more often. The art of being idle has scientifically backed benefits and psychologist Tony Crabbe would agree. In his book, *Busy: How to Thrive in a World of Too Much*, he explores how our brains are not machines, yet we have almost been conditioned to think of them as such since the Industrial Revolution and the introduction of technology. We are encouraged to think if we run them for longer, we get more out of them, but actually this is a false economy. Crabbe says that although the brain can deal with stress, it needs periods of recovery time, just like the body does for exercise. Crabbe says 'think, reflect; do, recover'.

I was particularly bad at this in my twenties. I literally went for it day in and day out. Eventually I noticed that my body had adjusted to this pace of life – and not in a good way! For 11 and half months of the year, from January 1st to the middle of December, I literally never got ill. Then after the last official selling day of the year for my company, which was mid-December, my body would literally collapse. For four years in a row I was ill at Christmas, and this was directly linked to the pace of work and a lot of the unnecessary 'busyness' I was creating in my life.

It nearly happened again in the pandemic of 2020 when everything went from being in control and growing to out of control, and we were working relentlessly to save the business. I found the transition from the physical world of meetings to the virtual world of having nearly tenfold the meetings in a week took time to get used to, like everyone else. Mentally I was doing more work in a week than I had ever done before and had to spend more time in my life than ever before performing, but this time behind a screen.

It was only after conversations with my coach when I started my first business, and more recently again with a slightly different approach, that things began to change. In the beginning, we started looking at my week with the lenses of an entrepreneur – if you're doing that, you're not doing this. We removed distractions gradually over a year and included focusing on building in time for rest. This became easy as time went on and I had a family because the rule I would make is no work at the weekend – *that's not to say family life isn't crazy at times, but I certainly now get a rest from the business.* Now what I do is linked to the Top Tip in this level, so I won't spoil it here, but it's been a game-changer for me over the last few years.

Work/life balance

Within the sphere of being busy and how to work effectively, we do need to consider all of the above and the part the elusive work/life balance plays in our lives. This phrase, which was around in the 70s/80s, has become something we all strive for. For working parents, it's finding the balance between earning money and spending time as a family. For some it will be finding time for their hobbies in between work. It is perhaps this change in perspective of work and leisure time which has meant those who are 'busy' are in fact complaining about their lack of leisure or family balance against the work they do.

The phrase work/life balance is bandied around, but we need to take it seriously, otherwise the consequences can be devastating – it can put our physical and mental health in jeopardy. A UCL study of 10,000 participants showed that those who work three or more hours longer than required had a 60 per cent higher risk of heart-related problems than those who didn't work overtime.[20] Some food for thought. People really need a no-blame culture and an environment in which they know that they can take a break without fear of seeming to not be pulling their weight (another great idiom). In the UK, 'three in five (60 per cent) say they work longer hours than they want and one in four (25 per cent) say they overwork by ten or more hours a week.'[21] That really isn't sustainable, and they certainly won't be working at their optimum.

---

20 https://thehappinessindex.com/employee-engagement/importance-of-work-life-balance

21 https://www.onrec.com/news/statistics-and-trends/stress-overwork-and-poor-work-life-balance-undermine-uk-job-quality

Being brilliantly busy

I believe we need to switch to using the term 'being brilliantly busy'. Being brilliantly busy is a term I came up with in the early days of my first business. Unlike in my previous role, as an entrepreneur I found myself once again with unbounded energy – I was never hitting the snooze button and I was jumping out of bed wanting to push the venture forward.

I was loving what I was doing and I found myself using these words naturally – being brilliantly busy. When I said that phrase to people, the reaction was always the same – a smile, a pause and then some internal reflection on why I entered the word 'brilliantly' before it. There might even occasionally be a slight bit of jealousy about how passionate I was about my job compared to their position. Nonetheless, it made people think.

I do wonder how often the word 'busy' is used by people doing jobs they love, compared to those who don't. I believe with people who love their jobs and seem to have that unbounded energy like a puppy, it is because their job is indeed linked to their passions. They've found their WHY in life and gone and also found a job which makes them tick, day in, day out. Many of us tend to fall into one of three camps:

1. You work in a job linked to your passion. Stop using the word busy – you're lucky! And you really are lucky because a survey in the UK determined that 85 per cent of us work in jobs we are unhappy with and 66 per cent are disengaged.[22] Are you in the fortunate 15 per cent?

---

22 https://techjury.net/blog/employee-engagement-statistics

2. You work in a job partly linked to your passion. A great example is a vocational career. Think about why you went into it, check your WHY is still relevant, and remind yourself of that.
3. Your work isn't linked to your passion at all. Time to begin to architect your path to your passion. If you're in this position, it might not necessarily be your fault, but if you're still in this position in years to come, then it will certainly be.

If you really want to change your mentality and create positive ripples, it's time to realise how important words like 'busy' are, and how sometimes the words you use actually begin to demonstrate to people on the outside what is going through your mind and what the state of your mentality is.

Bringing it all together

Becoming brilliantly busy means:

➤ you're more aware of the language you use and how it builds an impression
➤ you're spending your time on something linked to your passions
➤ you feel like you're using your time in the way that you want
➤ you create a sense of purpose around yourself every day
➤ you drive yourself to use every minute wisely each day.

So how can you move from being busy to brilliantly busy?

Top tip: Personal utilisation report

Anyone who says they're too busy and there isn't any way they can possibly find time in the week quite frankly needs to take a long hard look at themselves. No human being can say that they're running their week in the most efficient way – there is always time to be found.

I remember having this same argument once with a senior person who ran a large department within a multinational company – she claimed her 1000 people were so busy that any productive gains were impossible. I quickly proved her wrong by asking a few questions, such as: are there no processes you have which could be improved? Is everyone in the business familiar with the theory of marginal gains? Do you have any way of hearing all types of ideas? A member of her team, by chance, walked by the office and I decided to gamble and ask her if we could bring them in to ask them a question – if he claimed there was not a single productivity idea he had to save time, then I would leave the meeting. The person walking past happened to be a maintenance worker. We pulled him into the boardroom (after explaining he wasn't getting fired), and I asked him how long he had worked there – which was five years – and did he have any ideas at all that could be implemented to help him save time in the business. He then proceeded to explain a frustration he and other colleagues had at the queues in the canteen. He had no idea why they just didn't get a second or third till, allowing people to sit down and eat more quickly and get back to work. We quickly added up the potential time it could save and this particular leader ended up getting my point. The gamble worked!

Back to you. What you need to do is find time and start by analysing every moment of your day and week and looking for natural inefficiencies and the marginal gains you can apply to your own life. If you're unfamiliar with marginal gains, these are the small incremental improvements you can make, and the theory was partly made famous by the former British cycling coach Sir David Brailsford – this approach led the team to profound success in the Olympics. When he became head of British cycling in 2002, the team had almost no record of success: British cycling had only won a single gold medal in its 76-year history. That quickly changed under Sir Dave's leadership. At the 2008 Beijing Olympics, his squad won seven out of ten gold medals available in track cycling, and they matched the achievement at the London Olympics four years later.

By embracing this, we can move away from 'being busy' to a better mindset of 'being brilliantly busy' as you spend more time on the things you want to and consequently improve your state of mind.

I would highly encourage readers to begin by analysing your time with an online calendar. If you use one for work or managing your life, then build on this and note down everything you do. I don't mean entering a five-minute diary note for brushing your teeth, but potentially a diary entry for the first 60 minutes of your day as 'getting ready', which covers brushing your teeth, getting changed, etc. I would then fill up the rest of the day in a similar style and soon you will begin to see how you're spending chunks of your time, how (if needed) these could be reduced and indeed where some possible free chunks could be.

MON 18	TUE 19	WED 20	THU 21	FRI 22
Nursery Drop Off 7 – 8:15am				Voicenote/Chatsworth F 7:45 – 8:45am
Admin/Email 8:30 – 9:15am	Keynote SLIDES/PREP 8 – 9:45am	Pipeline Actions 7:30 – 10am	Write Shareholders Lett(	DH WORK Accounts (Gregor FYI) 8:45 – 10am
8b Weekly Comms. Mee 9:15 – 10am			8billionideas // Harrow I	
8billionideas and FRP A(	Catch Up with Becks, Al 9:45 – 10:30am	Confirmed - OneFourFive Meeting - Wonderland, 2-6 Boundary Row, London SE1 8HP 10am – 5pm LONDON Waterloo	Newstead Videos - Messa	RUN/LUNCH/KIDS 10 – 11:30am
Directors Meeting - Surbiton 10:30am – 1.30pm	Catch Up with Tara re: C 10:30 – 11:15am		Admin/Emails, 9:45am	
	Run/SHOWER/Lunch 11:15am – 12:30pm		Modelling Plan - 8billionid 8b x DND, David/Karen	Record Assembly, 11:30
			Prep for 1.15, 11am	
	Problem Wheel, 12:30pr		Catch Up with Dave Mor	Account Planning Sessi 12 – 1pm
	David, 8b to Call Nick A>		KEEP FREE 12 – 1:15pm	
Lunch/Travel 1:30 – 2:30pm	ROAR Project 1000 1:30 – 2:45pm 8billionideas		Catch Up with Mike & A(1:15 – 2pm	SHOP, 1pm
Admin/Email, 2:30pm			Granted // 8 Bibillionide: Commercial CEO Cadence	Prospect Work/Dubai Outreach 1:30 – 3pm
Catch Up with David/Ka	Pipeline Actions for the		TOBY, 2:45pm	
Weekly Cashflow & Fina	Variable Income Work, 3:1		Follow Up, 3:15pm	Handover \ Sales Team 3 – 3.45pm / 3 – 3.45pm
Chat with Clemmie, Cha	Harrow Bangkok Work, :		Follow Up Thank You - A 3:45 – 4:30pm	Record CS Proposal, 3:4
Variable Income Work PoA 4:30 – 5:45pm	URGENT - Dubai Standu		Chatsworth Proposals, -	Cashflow Call/Invoices 4:15 – 5:30pm ZOOM
	Client Emails 4:30 – 5:45pm		Asana Tidy Up, 5pm	
			Parent's Evening 5.40 – 6:25pm	

When I was growing my first business, I was getting frustrated at the lack of time I was having to build the 'pipeline' or new sales for the organisation. We decided to chunk up my diary like this to see how much time I had actually spent in the last month on activities related to this. Because everything was put into my diary from 'email management' to 'admin' to 'getting children ready' for nursery or school, we could actually work it out quite quickly. New sales accounted for less than five per cent of my weekly office hours, which was just too little, and we ended up actually making one of my executive assistants' KPIs to find time for me to spend nearer to 20 per cent of my time on the pipeline.

Even more recently, we segmented my time between the hours of 8 am and 5.30 pm into these areas:

Personal
➤ childcare
➤ running
➤ lunch
➤ personal appointments

Time away
➤ holidays

Internal
➤ Asana – our project management tool
➤ supporting deliverables
➤ internal catch-ups (non-director)
➤ director catch-ups
➤ writing
➤ external coaching
➤ pipeline building
➤ strategy
➤ personal training
➤ investor time
➤ speaking and preparation
➤ interviews

External
➤ potential new clients
➤ existing clients
➤ networking
➤ favours/support

Other
➤ empty time

It didn't take long to see some of the problems right in front of me. I needed to review my internal responsibilities and become more externally focused. I needed to create more empty time to just think and not fill every second. I needed to see what I could delegate to buy back even more time. This kind of analysis takes time, but it's fascinatingly insightful and I would highly recommend it. This is some sample analysis from a month:

What was my conclusion after seeing this?

Utilisation of David's Time Per Week

MASTER (DO NOT EDIT) Month of June	Day 1 8am - 5.30pm	Day 2 8am - 5.30pm	Day 3 8am - 5.30pm	Day 4 8am - 5.30pm	Day 5 8am - 5.30pm	TOTAL	% of Overall Time
Personal							
Childcare	30	0	60	60	0	150	1.36%
Run	90	90	90	90	210	570	5.18%
Lunch	135	120	120	165	105	645	5.86%
Personal Appointments	0	0	0	30	60	90	0.82%
	255	210	270	345	375	1455	13.22%
Holidays							
Time away	0	540	0	0	0	540	4.91%
	0	540	0	0	0	540	4.91%
Internal Workload							
Asana/Admin	305	60	45	150	125	685	6.22%
Deliverables Support	30	0	510	135	100	775	7.04%
Internal catch ups (non Director)	245	240	90	90	335	1000	9.09%
Director catch ups	245	135	60	135	75	650	5.91%
Writing	45	0	0	45	0	45	0.41%
External coaching	165	225	300	180	60	930	8.45%
Pipeline building	105	210	465	0	225	1005	9.13%
Strategy	240	210	135	275	165	1025	9.31%
Personal training	0	30	0	0	0	30	0.27%
Investor Time	0	0	0	15	0	15	0.14%
Speaking (+ prep)	60	150	240	0	155	605	5.50%
Interviews	0	0	0	0	0	0	0.00%
	0	1260	1845	1025	1240	5370	48.80%
External Workload							
Potential new clients	30	0	0	195	60	285	2.59%
Existing clients	90	435	210	135	375	1245	11.31%
Networking (LinkedIn)	30	45	60	30	30	195	1.77%
Favours/support	0	0	0	0	0	0	0.00%
	150	480	270	360	465	1725	15.67%
No time allocated	160	120	210	195	195	880	8.00%
	160	120	210	195	195	880	8.00%
Outside of 8am - 5.30pm	480	225	210	120	0	1035	9.40%
	480	225	210	120	0	1035	9.40%
TOTAL	1045	2835	2805	2045	2275	11005	

Total Hours 183.42

Pie chart:
- Outside of working hours 9.4%
- Personal 13.2%
- Holidays 4.9%
- No time allocated 8.0%
- External workload 15.7%
- Internal workload 48.8%

Far too much time focused on internal workload. The goal would be to reduce this by 15–20 per cent and double my external commitments; however, without this analysis, it wouldn't have been so obvious.

You might begin to tell that I'm a little relentless on this topic and sometimes take it even to the next level if that's possible. Albeit it might sound silly, another regular slot in my diary was '15-minute coffee run' to nip out at the start of the day to grab a coffee from a local shop. When I saw this slot, I just thought to myself that I should buy a good coffee machine and could make one to take with me at the start of the day – so I did. It might not look or sound like a big saving of time, but it actually is – see below.

➤ 15 minutes a day x 365 days = 5475 minutes
➤ 5475 minutes divided by 60 = 91.25 hours
➤ 91.25 hours divided by 24 = 3.80 days

This is exactly what I mean by 'finding time' no matter the length; it can help you focus on what you really want to focus on. This one 15 minutes a day saving over a year would give me nearly four calendar days back to be brilliant and busy on what I'm passionate about – in terms of usable daytime it's actually about 11 days' worth. I do believe people are always 'busy' but could easily find time back with some simple analysis. With a few shifts in thinking like this, you will stop feeling busy and start feeling *brilliantly* busy and be in a better frame of mind as you attempt to create ripples daily.

This approach to thinking about your time and busyness won't guarantee you success, but what it will do is certainly give you a greater chance of it. A greater chance to be able to think, to make better decisions and ultimately create more positive ripples.

Reflections

Being brilliantly busy is a good thing, otherwise you'll be not-so brilliantly bored. But it really does start by valuing your own time and others, and then *directing it into areas that you really want to focus on in your life*. But be careful when using the word 'busy': it can affect your mentality. I'd be surprised if any world-class performers out there, in whatever they do, see themselves as being busy. *They might however say that they are terrifically tired because they're brilliantly busy pursuing a dream or a vision relentlessly!*

As you reflect on this level, think about what you're busy doing with your life. Think about how you say the word and think about how you can begin to find time and free yourself up a little. Imagine what you could achieve if you found an extra day in your week. Don't be a busy bee for the sake of it as nobody likes busybodies and you'll also soon be a knackered bee with no impact. Get busy doing something you want. *Value your time. Value every second of it.*

Takeaways

➤ For many people the word 'busy' has negative connotations, but it can be positive too – it can be a sign of your success.

➤ There is a difference between being busy and being productive – work smarter, not harder!

➤ Don't use being busy as an excuse not to do things; prioritised and managed properly, there's always time to be brilliantly busy.

➤ Value your time – every second of it!

Time to get ready for Level 4 and consider the impact of failures on our ability to make ripples.

Level 4

The F Word

Failure is just part and parcel of life – it happens. It can be a positive thing, but only if you reflect and adapt as a result – otherwise it's not failure, it's just stupidity. It's about learning from the experiences which might be deemed failures to go into the next experience in a better, stronger position. Some of the ripples you create might not lead to the outcome that you want but the very next day you'll have the opportunity to make a new set of ripples again and learn from those mistakes of yesterday.

When we talk about failure, what we are really talking about are those times when your success was based upon an end goal that was to be achieved, and your mindset has led you to believe that you failed. Not that they don't serve a purpose, but these 'failures' don't define us as people. In this level I want to turn the notion of failure on its head so you're able to move forward without it hanging over you, being fearless in the next challenge. I believe that this is critical for creating ripples as failure allows reflection and with reflection come lessons learned, a renewed sense of purpose and the ability, now with experience, to make more positive ripples in the future.

Embrace failure

Failure. It's been a buzzword over the last decade, but we now seem to have turned the tide and are facing it head on: no longer is failure something to be afraid of, but something to be embraced!

There are lots of examples where we use the word 'failure' – in exams, driving tests and sport, to name a few; it's even used in parenting. In all instances, however, we should look for the positive and try to view it as a learning experience.

Let's begin then with its actual meaning: 'Failure is the state or condition of not meeting a desirable or intended objective, and may be viewed as the opposite of success.'[23] Right, there is the problem: that it can be seen as the opposite to success. In fact, failure could be seen as being *necessary* to success. Just like Einstein said, 'Success is failure in progress.' So how do we change our perception of failure? How can we turn it into a positive? How can failure make things better?

Confusing, isn't it? I want to break this down, take some of the myths away and give you the chance as a reader to explore this against the background of your own story, allowing *you* to determine your own definition of failure,

---

23 https://en.wikipedia.org/wiki/Failure

and whether in fact you are able to let go and switch your thinking. Let me tell you a story where some may perceive the outcome as a failure, but I saw it as a learning opportunity.

One major lesson for me was from the first major sales deal I led early in my career – I touched on this earlier in the book. For 18 months I had built a relationship, managed the client and built a very substantial deal for the company I was working for. Personally, it also had a life-changing amount of commission for me. I put plans in place to control every aspect I could and to anticipate changes to that plan from a client's perspective. As the deal got into eight-figure territory it was getting more and more focus internally, so I knew I had to be prepared. I created a detailed 'Win Plan', which is a plan to make sure I secured the deal, as well as a 'What Could Go Wrong Plan', in which I tried to think of everything and anything that could prevent the deal from happening in the final financial quarter of the year. This wasn't a process in place at the company for big deals like this; it was something I created.

The day before the deal was due to complete, I received the official thumbs-up from our client that the purchase order was raised and it had now been signed off by the chief financial officer. In the morning we would receive the contracts. Cue a huge sigh of relief from my perspective. However, something was telling me to not celebrate too early.

Early the next morning I had a message from the client saying we needed to speak. His message was at 5 am, which wasn't too unusual as I knew he was an early riser, but the tone of it did worry me. We got the team onto a 7.30 am call and the client announced that the deal was gone. In a bizarre twist of events, despite their CFO signing off the deal, a basic accounting error had occurred and the CAPEX (capital expenditure) allocated to this project was never actually allocated. The CFO and the chief innovation officer had been told that they had X amount to spend, but an accountant actually forgot to allocate the money months before this deal was due to close. So, although the client thought that they had the eight-figure sum to spend, they actually had *nothing*. There was no money in the budget!

As you can imagine, my heart sank. Within 24 hours, I went from thinking I had closed a career-changing deal; to there being nothing. It was a massive blow to take and within a few hours I was being called into our head office to explain the situation. This type of ending didn't normally happen. Losing a deal to a competitor is one thing, but your client messing up their internal accounting systems and no one being any the wiser, even their CFO, was something else completely!

Luckily, my bosses understood the due diligence I had gone through and some great people management from them helped pick me up so I could focus on the bigger picture and maintain the client relationship to make sure I closed it in the next financial year. And I did, but my targets were changed because now the business expected it; there was no way they would pay out on the commission they would have done when they hadn't expected a deal of this size.

When I reflect now on this perceived 'failure', I just see lots of lessons – the main one being, 'It's never done until it's done.' I was proud to have tried everything I could have and honestly would not have done anything differently in terms of managing the deal. The only thing I would have changed would have been not to let my thoughts move to a good place until the contract was officially signed.

A key lesson for me was learning that failure is not the opposite of success but, in fact, *the opposite of trying*. That's an interesting thought and it changed my perception of what failure is – if you haven't even tried then you have failed.

Another example from me has been the failed attempts at raising capital for the businesses that I've run. We grow up in a media world hearing about the successes of entrepreneurs and investment won on programmes like *Dragons' Den* which can see the creation of an overnight success. But the reality of it is the opposite. Gaining investment is difficult and often requires countless conversations before you have developed your value proposition and your pitch and found the right person or firm to back your business at the right time. There are so many things stacked against you when looking to raise capital, such as timing, personal preferences, market conditions and competitors, to name a few, such that when you go into a round of investment you require for your business, you have to take failure as part of the process. As an individual who has raised money through private crowdfunding, public crowdfunding, angel and private equity investment, believe me – it's part of the process. But each time you do fail, you must learn, adapt and go again.

Perceptions of failure

Michelle Obama describes failure as 'a feeling long before it becomes an actual result. It's vulnerability that breeds with self-doubt and then is escalated, often deliberately, by fear'.[24] And it's that feeling that keeps us tied to failure.

---

24 Obama, M. (2018). *Becoming*. Penguin.

We have a physical response to it, usually the fight-or-flight response, and even a third – the freeze. These reactions are hard wired into the body, so no wonder it's easy for us to 'feel' failure as a physical response. Those feelings of anxiety, depression or sadness are turning points (and if you haven't felt them, then you are probably already thinking along the lines of everything as a learning experience).

Although we often feel a physical response to failure, a lot of how we cope with failure is down to how we *perceive* it. As Abraham Lincoln once said, 'My great concern is not whether you have failed, but whether you are content with your failure.' This attitude can help us align our perception of what failure is to us and how much importance we want to place on it – it's more about how happy we are with the outcome. Rather than feel shame if you believe that it hasn't gone well, you need to progress beyond that and make the gains you planned for yourself.

A lot of what is discussed in this book is about business, but fear of failure can permeate all aspects of life, some with equally high stakes, such as in sport. Jake Humphrey, the television journalist, has conducted a series of podcasts with high-performing individuals. One of the things he ascertained through these interviews is how these successful people have dealt with their perception of failure. Jonny Wilkinson, Rugby World Cup winner for England in 2003, explained that one of the factors that maintained his drive has been having *no regrets*. This is important because, even if you feel like there have been times when something has failed, if you don't regret the decisions you made, then you can move on from it and *begin learning from it*.

Another high-profile sportsman, Ben Ainslie, the most successful sailor in Olympic history, said in his interview that focusing on the bad aspects of an experience is *where learning begins*. It seems then that acknowledging failure – or aspects of an experience that didn't go as we planned – is a healthy admission; but the important thing is not dwelling on it, which will help us move on more quickly. If we spend too long analysing our failures then that becomes the sole focus and can hold us back; acknowledging it and then being ready to move on to success, however, is far more beneficial.

Responding to failure as part of a team

So far we've looked at failure on an individual basis. What about when we're part of a team – how do we approach failure, especially from a position of leadership? Do you recognise it at all? If so, how do you communicate failure to your team? Is the failure just an opinion rather than a fact? What kind of ripples might this create? It's not always easy knowing what to do but it's worth coming back to Ben Ainslie and the three non-negotiables he lists in his podcast interview when working in a high-powered team:

➤ commitment
➤ resilience
➤ team ethos.

The great thing about being in a team where everyone is equally committed is that responsibility is shared, so no one should feel an overriding burden on their own. This shared commitment helps develop resilience, the ability to accept difficulties and move on. This means failure is less of an issue, but more important is how a team pulls together, learns from it and moves forward – that's a good team ethos.

From a personal point of view, when I look back on my first business, I believe we made one big failure as a team and that was to take our eyes off the ball when it came to quality – we sometimes fell into the trap of delivering 'good but not great' work. This wasn't a deliberate choice, but it's what happened as we had to continually focus on winning business, to be able to pay wages and keep the lights on as a developing start-up. However, it took far too long for the penny to drop and realise that what we were doing was making work harder for ourselves in the future. Winning your first client is the hardest. Once we have won them, we need to retain them forever! Our retention rate was brilliant, but it could have been better. With a deep focus on our work and pushing every part of our operations and delivery team to produce world-class products and services, repeat business would be a no-brainer. We failed at having an equal balance focusing on new projects and business alongside quality. I'll never make that mistake again and in the business I run now, the entire team attends a 'quality' call each week looking at all client feedback from the previous seven days, and we make sure an action is put in place on anything that can improve our services and products for the future.

The home team

There are different types of teams, of course. One that you might not think of in that sense, but one we learn a lot from, is our families. One of the intangible failures

I mentioned at the beginning of this level, for example, was failure as a parent. It might seem an odd example to cite, especially for those who haven't had children, but it will probably strike a chord for those who have. It's a controversial phrase; luckily, I think society is stamping out that feeling of failure where parenting is concerned – but it's hard for a parent not to occasionally feel a sense of failure in some regard.

My wife Jenny and I felt it with our son Toby when he was young. Toby didn't say his first word until he was three years old. He was a happy little chap, but all we could get out of him throughout that period was babble. Everyone we spoke to – friends/family – said you have nothing to worry about, he will be fine, sometimes they're late bloomers, and we just thought that would be the case. We did a little bit of Googling but not hours of research as the constant reassurance from everyone, including a doctor, at the time was, 'You have nothing to worry about'. But for a period of time I wished I had pushed harder and got more medical opinions.

The penny really dropped when he was two and a half and he was allowed to start 'Little Kickers', which is football lessons at the weekend. For the first time, outside of the nursery, we could see Toby lined up against children of a similar age, and something wasn't quite right. He wasn't naughty, but he wasn't engaged. Every other child would sit, kick and listen when the coach spoke, but Toby just seemed to be happy looking around and not listening. It was by chance that a friend mentioned that the most common issue with delayed speech is something to do with their ears, but we had got his ears checked at one of his tests and nothing came back – the problem was it wasn't done properly. We decided to push and go again and at three years old, we were eventually told he needed an ear operation. Our little lad, for the first three years of his life, had effectively been going around with blocked ears and partial hearing. By luck, our babysitter's dad was an ear, nose and throat consultant and helped get something booked in quickly. Grommets were introduced, an operation cleared things up and within six weeks he was talking. It was a remarkable turnaround, and when you now see him with his school friends you wouldn't have any idea; however, for a while my wife and I did feel like we had messed up, had failed, but over time we have come to terms with it.

The problem is, you don't get a manual when you become a parent. Many people have tried creating them – there are countless parenting books available, each with their own way of doing things. They have their place, but on the whole, it's almost impossible to have a rule of thumb for a race of unique beings – no two babies are the same. Of course, we feel safer if someone else tells us what to do, especially when we have no experience of it. We want to 'do the right thing', but rarely is there in fact one right thing. And knowing if we are doing the right thing or not is what can cause emotional turmoil because it's what decides if we have 'failed' or not.

Learning how to fail

A lot of what we learn about failure, and how we react to it, comes from how we were brought up by our parents. For example, over the years we have shied away from allowing children to 'fail' at anything and instead try to treat them all the same. That can have many different outcomes – good and bad.

One well-known term for this kind of parenting is 'parachute' or 'helicopter' parenting, where well-meaning parents try to protect their children from failure. However, this can have unintended negative effects as it's important for their development that children fail and are able to learn from this. They need to develop a tolerance of failure so that they can deal with the inevitability of it in life; this can help them with self-esteem and reduce anxiety. This might seem surprising given that avoidance of failure suggests this has the same outcome.

An amazing friend and client has an alternative approach which I admire. What she recommends is 'trampoline' parenting, which she has discussed in a TEDx talk. This means that, when your child is falling, or indeed failing, you let it happen and let them bounce back up. It's a style that my wife and I attempt to adopt with our children, but it's not always easy at times.

The difficulty then is how we teach that to children and help them develop the right mindset as they enter adulthood. The Child Mind Institute suggests empathy and using our own experiences as a way to model behaviour. If we can communicate the times when we ourselves have struggled, faced failure and fought back, we give them the tools to fight failure throughout life. It goes back to that thought process that *it's not the failure that's important, but how you deal with it that matters*.

Bringing it all together

Embracing failure will ultimately allow you to create positive ripples if you reflect and learn from it. It's a good thing because:

> ➤ you accept failure as part of life
> ➤ you learn to see the good in difficult situations
> ➤ you use it to fuel your next set of challenges
> ➤ it can change your perspective on the world, helping you to see the bigger picture
> ➤ you can't achieve great things without ever failing along the way.

So how do we look back on failures from the past, embrace them and move forward to create positive ripples in the future?

Top tip: The Failure Elevator Pitch

You've probably not heard of a failure elevator pitch before, the reason being it's not what we do on a typical day. How often do we stop and think about our failures, and then summarise them like an elevator pitch? It seems like a strange thing to do but this is exactly what I want you to do, and be clear in articulating them.

In our round table discussions, I often like to ask students, 'What is your biggest failure?' I'm keen to see if they can not only talk about it, but also to see if, as individuals, they learned anything from it. I remember one time asking 12 prefects at a brilliant school this question and then hitting the stopwatch on my watch to see who would say something first. There were eight minutes of silence before a student finally decided to tell me something about losing on a sporting field. When I asked them about their successes, in contrast, hands were up, grades were shared, certificates and prizes won, but it just made me think how uncomfortable people are with this topic. It's not just students, but adults too; maybe try asking this question in a team meeting in your organisation or business soon and see if you get the same reaction.

Just like when we talk about our successes, being clear on your failures and the lessons learned is critical. Not only is it a good reflection exercise in terms of self-development but it always comes up in interviews, so it's really worth doing. Look back over your life and select up to three failures which have really shaped your view of the world. What were they? What happened to you? What impact did it have and how did it change you?

Write them down and use figures or statistics to stress the impact if they warrant it. Once you're done, you should have three soundbites which could look something like this:

When I was 24, I led a $12.5m deal which failed to close on the last day of the financial year for the organisation I worked with. Because the deal wasn't closed, I didn't hit my yearly goals, and neither did anyone in my team. It had a devastating impact on my confidence at the time as well as my short- to medium-term financial security. However, I learned that because I was transparent before the deal and indeed after the deal with my bosses, there was nothing I could do. In the future, and since then, I've never celebrated a deal or a win until a contract was signed. It taught me to be even more cautious when managing clients.

This reflection exercise will help you to be clearer on your failures in the past and be a constant reminder and driver to create positive ripples in the future. Successes of course define you, but I think failures do more; you learn more from a loss than a win and you learn more from a knock-back than from moving forward. Failures help you build your experience and your character, and they ultimately help you to make better ripples in the future... *if you learn from them!*

Reflections

If you think back to your own childhood, what was failure to you? How did your parents view failure? How did you feel? How did you change your thoughts about failure as an adult? This level gives you the opportunity to reset your thoughts on failure and make a life for yourself as you choose to see it without having those negative influences holding you back. Think about where you are now or perhaps where you want to be. History has given us many examples of individuals who have had to keep pushing through the challenges to achieve success like Dyson and his 5,000+ prototypes.[25]

Hopefully you are starting to see how our understanding and attitudes towards risk have changed over time and, even now, people perceive it differently. In all aspects of life we are faced with failures or, if you prefer, learning experiences. What I have shown you is that really it's a paradox: when we take this stigma out of failure, then it can't be seen as failure anymore. This is your journey to steer as you wish, but be clear with what your vision for success is. For you to create impactful ripples in the future, you need to learn from the positive and negative ones from the past.

---

25 See https://nymag.com/vindicated/2016/11/james-dyson-on-5-126-vacuums-that-didnt-work-and-1-that-did.html

Takeaways

➤ Acknowledge failure, but don't dwell on it.
➤ Don't view failure as the opposite of success, but in fact, the opposite of trying.
➤ When we take the stigma out of failure, then it can't be seen as failure anymore.

You're now more than halfway there – let's move away from failure and talk about curiosity!

Level 5

Constantly Curiously Creative

What comes to mind first when you think of the word 'curious'? Does it make you think of being inquisitive, or is it something strange and unusual?

Curiosity can lead us down the most interesting and rewarding pathways. Being constantly curious can fuel the adventurer inside of us and take us to places that are often hard to imagine. If you add a bit of creativity to whatever you might be curious about, you may find you stumble across new solutions to all sorts of problems, tiny, small or big – this is often how inventions are born. Be prepared to be bravely curious, and indeed creative, if you want to make explosive ripples.

In this level we are exploring the inquisitive meaning of the word and I want to show how being curious can help you make explosive ripples – ripples that can change the culture of an organisation, new business or a community that you're part of. We should all be lifelong curious learners and the only way to do that is by asking questions, following up on the answers and getting people to ask questions of us. Learning is a two-way street and helps us not only create ripples which impact others' attitudes but can also expand their knowledge and wisdom.

Spark your curiosity

Curiosity is a natural instinct – it's a drive for learning to fill the gaps in our knowledge and understanding. However, this natural instinct is squashed for many because our education systems aren't perfectly set up for curiosity to flourish – they take a one-size-fits-all approach in pretty much every corner of the world.

This is the long-term challenge in education: we will never have a perfect education system until every child can go through a personalised learning journey while at school – which might seem far-fetched but with some creative thinking and the use of technology it is possible.

Education is close to my heart. I've been involved in many think tanks trying to solve problems and my philosophy is relatively straightforward.

Currently, the majority of schools globally operate like coffee shops but with hardly anything on the menu (and not because they don't want to offer more). Children are walking in and probably being served black coffee, white coffee and some might offer green tea! However, these aren't everyone's chosen drinks. Nowadays everyone wants something different: a cappuccino with a caramel shot, a double espresso in a china cup, a hot chocolate with three marshmallows, etc. We've all got different tastes and needs, and this is no different for students walking into a school; however, their learning pathways are determined by the parameters schools are under. They pretty much all have to follow the same pathway. I will welcome the day when every child has a different pathway bespoke to them and their passions, which we can track, revisit, redirect and alter throughout their life. There is no reason at all why a teacher can't stand up in front of 30 children with 30 independent lessons happening at the same time with the use of technology and personalised learning – it might just take us a few decades to get there!

This is why it can be frustrating for educators when students don't want to learn what is being taught, yet it doesn't mean that those students don't want to learn about their subject – it's just not personal or relatable to them yet. A great example is a young student who wants to be a footballer, but hates maths. To many they see there is no link, but to me there is a link between every subject and every industry or job in the world. If you want to be an outstanding footballer, having an appreciation for angles will help with set plays, percentages with performance analysis and, of course, numbers when it comes to contract negotiations!

If the natural instinct is to learn, then we need to allow people to follow what makes them curious. This is something leaders need to be aware of too when working with their teams, giving people the room to be curious and thinking about what sparks their curiosity. Think about the last time you learned how to do something – it doesn't have to be a university degree; it could be a simple online course or just something that furthered your knowledge. Anything you have put your mind to will have been done to enhance yourself on a deeper level – you were curious about something and wanted to find out more. How did you feel when you embarked on it? How did you feel during the process? How did you feel afterwards? No doubt you felt empowered and rewarded, which then led on to higher engagement. This is one of the benefits of businesses and organisations really focusing on their innovation and creativity strategy as it has a direct impact on these key areas.

Being creative doesn't have to mean being artistic or making things out of paper and plastic. Being creative is actually the ability to find patterns in things and find new ways of working. This can be applied to any way of working from computers to drama to sport – there is creativity in everything. Forgive me for the second football example within this level, but even 'the wall' used in football is a good example. The story goes that, in 1957, the Northern Ireland team were looking at options to try and stop the Italians. In a biography of the footballer Danny Blanchflower, he is quoted as saying, 'We tried to do things that nobody else had ever thought of. We had to because they were better sides. We put up the first wall at a free kick. They seemed to be frightened by the tactic. It did have its teething problems though. The referee had never seen it either, so when the Italians picked up the ball and moved it five yards away from the wall and shot into the net, he gave it a goal!'[26] This first attempt was the equivalent of a prototype by a new business and now you see it used in every game around the world. In more recent years you may have seen people lying down behind the wall to cover the gap along the floor when the players jump – another example of further creativity.

Successful people will find all sorts of different techniques

---

26 Bowler, D. (1998). *Danny Blanchflower: A Biography*. Orion.

to enhance themselves; for example, speed reading, listening to podcasts or talking to competitors to give their creative juices an edge, seek a marginal gain and become better. It's why you hear so many sports stories of coaches going to watch other teams in other sports all around the world. The latest I heard was Gareth Southgate, the England football manager, spending time with Toto Wolfe at the Formula One Mercedes team and learning techniques about how to build that team atmosphere beyond just the 11 footballers on the pitch representing their country. Formula One, it's easy to forget, is not just the driver in the car but the hundreds if not thousands of people in the garage which makes the driver's performance possible. One example is that Toto realised how much needed to change from the moment he walked into Mercedes – he was so unimpressed with old coffee cups and the fact they had out of date newspapers in reception. It didn't feel world class to him.

If you need any more persuading, research even shows that curious people are happier. Eric Barker, science author and researcher, did a study with 97 college students over 21 days and found that on 'days when they were more curious, people who were high in trait curiosity reported more frequent growth-oriented behaviours, and greater presence of meaning, search for meaning, and life satisfaction'. He also found that the greater their curiosity, the longer the period it benefited them.[27]

Not just that, but they were also calmer and less anxious. In a similar way that positive people will find opportunities in the most unlikely of places, curious people will find something interesting even in seemingly

---

27 www.businessinsider.com/whats-the-connection-between-curiosity-and-happiness-2011-9

boring situations. Do what others aren't doing. There isn't a dull moment for curious people; they are always showing an interest in what's around them.

Lifelong learning and 24/7 learning

If we think of ourselves as being lifelong learners, we can see how education up to university stage (if people choose it) is really only a small part of our education as a whole. Learning is an everyday process in all aspects of life and opportunities to be curious and learn are everywhere. I would genuinely like to see 'lifelong learning' go beyond a phrase people like to use and be actually implemented, along with 24/7 learning. Let me break this down for different age groups.

Children: I believe every child should go to two schools – a physical school and a virtual one. Why? Children are at school for 15 per cent of their waking hours. Their physical school gives them that opportunity to build connections, have a sense of belonging and learn key knowledge, but why can't they have access outside of school hours to world-class extracurricular and life skills learning in the virtual world? It's definitely possible with the use of technology.

Adults (*and I'll lump all adults into this*): Why is it that learning stops at 18? It might extend a little for a degree, and a few might do a masters and then it's down to you. It's down to you to do free online courses, or it's down to you to persuade your work to pay for a course you're desperate to go on. I personally think we should be thinking really big and every adult should have access to learning in their community and every adult should be enrolled in a local college or establishment to have access to education whenever they want. The inspirational workshop. The world-class speaker. The course to help them manage the virtual world. If every adult was part of their local college and it was the norm that we were all enrolled somewhere, would people use it? Of course they would. Would it help them be more productive at work? Of course it would. Would it help them start new businesses? Of course it would. Yes, we might all have to pay for it out of our taxes, but we could all benefit and it would certainly help an economy build world-class businesses, products and services. I'm not sure anyone will be ambitious enough in any government around the world to think as big as this in my lifetime, though. If they did, lifelong learning would actually be real and we would be capitalising more time in our efforts to make it a 24/7 exercise, and not for a few hours of our lives as a child.

Creating the right conditions for curiosity

To be curious and creative, to develop new ideas, you sometimes need the right conditions to facilitate it. In his book *Where Good Ideas Come From* (Penguin, 2010), Steven Johnson explores how 'connections can facilitate ideas'. As a science writer he looks at life from its very early beginnings, when life began as carbon before it connected with other atoms and new life emerged. He moves through the history of how we have come to get to where we are, especially from a technological aspect, and how everything had to start simply before evolving into more complex organisms or, indeed, ideas. For many inventors, they may appear to have had an epiphany, but in actual fact it's been a learning process and they are more likely to have been developing an idea, building layer upon layer over time. There are many layers to a final idea – prototypes, inevitable failures, feedback and other environmental changes – that were not part of the idea in the first place, but which have a direct impact on the final product/service. 'Both evolution and innovation tend to happen within the bounds of the *adjacent possible*, in other words the realm of possibilities available at any given moment.'[28]

Think about the various successful platforms and apps that have been established over the last decade or so; these wouldn't have been successful if they had been developed earlier because they wouldn't have had the right environment in which the ideas could develop fully. Platforms like eBay, for example, needed online selling functions and a way to connect with people en masse. This doesn't mean that these successful businesses aren't continuing to develop – quite the opposite. The founders are still curious about how to solve ongoing issues, and that is inevitable where technology is concerned, which then drives their creativity – and so they develop better systems. Johnson makes some interesting comparisons between the natural world and our developed world. Take this example: 'Beavers fell trees that rot and attract woodpeckers to drill nesting holes in them. But once the woodpeckers have left, these holes are occupied by songbirds. The woodpecker has also created a platform.'

He continues: 'Platforms often stack on top of each other, meaning that one platform provides the foundation for even more platforms, which again produce countless new innovations.' The synergy is hard to ignore. It seems even more relevant that our natural environment provides a basis for the right things to happen at the right time and

---

28 https://medium.com/key-lessons-from-books/the-key-lessons-from-where-good-ideas-come-from-by-steven-johnson-1798e11becdb

that we have these building blocks. The *curiosity* to be part of that innovation in the first place is where it's at.

His conclusion is all about creating opportunities for a 'hunch' to happen. A hunch, he writes, is a non-crystallised thought or suggestion which, when it collides with other hunches, leads to a crystallised idea – and that's how good ideas are generated. Ideas are never just generated in one moment but need that opportunity and time to collide with other ideas. I saw it for myself with my first business. It took two years of ideas really developing and colliding before the actual idea formed. Since then, there have probably been a thousand further hunches on top of the first hunch, which has then led our business to where it is today.

The challenge in an organisation is creating opportunities for these hunches to happen. Companies like the idea of encouraging creativity but lack the real understanding that it must begin with creating the appropriate environments for hunches and then ideas to develop. Too often I see companies' strategies for generating good ideas being formed around the following:

➤ Suggestion box: someone, somewhere will think it's a good idea to put a box up in the office to collect ideas. However, these are never utilised and the only thing they actually collect is dust.

➤ Open-door policy: leaders will often announce that they have an open-door policy and employees can come in any time to share an idea. Although this is said with good intent, an employee has to have great courage to do this, and great timing, as leaders are often busy!

➤ Think tank sessions: you will also see organisations dedicate time on training days to solving problems or generating ideas in the form of a 'think tank', which is effectively when you put a collection of people together under pressure with a finite amount of time to come up with something (well, that's my definition!). What happens on these occasions is that poor ideas are formed and actually more often than not never acted on. Why? Because the documentation and implementation process isn't followed after these meetings as people get back to their busy day jobs, and ideas and innovation are once again just buzzwords.

Worse than those three common ways you see organisations attempt to innovate is what happens when a good idea is actually shared – you see the Ebbinghaus Forgetting Curve kicking in. This theory suggests that if an idea isn't written down and shared upon creation, over time it will be forgotten; surprisingly this happens all the time because organisations are busy places. There is always the next meeting. Always the next priority. Always a time when an employee is on holiday. Then suddenly an employee moves on and takes that great idea with them.

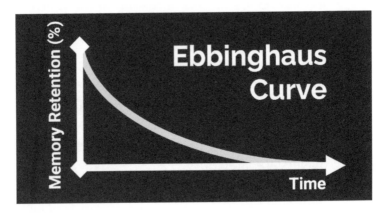

The best thing an organisation can do to nurture creativity is to stop and think about what it is doing to allow hunches to collide and then what systems are in place to be determined enough to make it happen. It doesn't need to be any more complicated than that.

Curiosity killed the cat – or did it?

On the flip side, is there a downside to being too curious? We've all heard of the phrase 'curiosity killed the cat' to warn people off asking meddlesome questions. It is often implied as a sign of nosiness rather than inquisitiveness and intelligence, but perhaps that is a misinterpretation. We can sometimes be very possessive of facts and reluctant to share, so anyone deemed to be asking things they shouldn't is automatically dismissed. There is also the perception that by asking questions it might be perceived that we just haven't made an effort to look first, and that there has to be some responsibility for thinking before speaking.

I coined a phrase once about people being 'brain lazy' for this exact moment: when they would ask people questions or ask for something when they could find it out themselves or go on a little hunt to get it. I noticed it happening in my first business when we were in a studio office, and most of it was around the use of technology. How do I get this piece of software on my laptop? Does anyone know the button for this? Where can I find this document? Simple, unharmful questions, but all of them are brain lazy if the individual has not tried to answer it themselves.

It might seem a little harsh from me, but actually this type of interruption by an employee of another employee can be incredibly disruptive for individuals and for the business. Being dyslexic, I might be in the zone, and when responding to a 'brain lazy' question, even for a few seconds, it might take me 10–15 minutes to get back into the flow. If you sit in an open office and you ask something like this of the team, you're then impacting others. I gradually stamped it out by responding with comments such as, 'What do you think the answer is? Have you spent any time looking to solve it? Have you Googled it?' My point was quickly made.

One of the team mentioned that he used to work in a software company and everyone had a sand timer on their desk. When faced with a problem, they would try to find the answer out for ten minutes and then ask if they were still stuck. I liked this idea a lot! When all sources have been exhausted, employees must then be confident to ask; however, an effort to try and find out the answer first is key.

Fearless curiosity

Amy Edmonson, the author, is known for her philosophy around fearless thinking. She is an advocate for encouraging organisations to create environments where individuals can be fearless as she believes this is the best way for innovation to really flourish. I agree with this, but there is a fine line between fearlessness and recklessness. Fearlessness must be when you act without fear of the repercussions that might come – you might fail at this but you won't lose your job; or you might not make great progress, but any progress is good. Recklessness is acting without thought, causing waste or damage.

Fearless curiosity is what I think really needs to be encouraged. Encouraging people to ask good questions (not brain-lazy ones), challenge the status quo, to go and learn what other members of their team do to gain appreciation of their job.

However, asking questions can be deemed as being nosey. It can be deemed as meddling where it needs to be the opposite. Why? I believe so many people go through their day jobs not always fully understanding what's going on around them or asking for clarity. We seem ashamed to ask out of embarrassment or fear of what the reaction would be. The problem with this is no one wins – the employee or the employer.

Let me give you an example. In the early days of the business, I once asked everyone whether or not they knew our mission statement, knowing that not everyone did. Plenty of nods and not a single person being brave enough to say that they weren't sure and ask what it was. They did what they thought I wanted and just said yes. I then gave them all a piece of paper and asked them to write it down and suddenly it was like a room of school children panicking before a test. Only ten per cent of them got it correct. To be honest, I wasn't fussed at how many didn't know it, as it had changed once or twice in our early days, but I *was* fussed at how no one put their hand up and asked what it was. I explained that was what was disappointing to me and if we were to grow, an environment of fearless curiosity would be required. Never feel ashamed to ask a question and never say 'yes' if you don't mean it. I'm glad to say it was a little turning point for our team and it's something I still advocate today. No question is genuinely a bad question. It's only a bad question if you know the answer!

Being constantly curious

This leads me to think that with all of this curiosity and creativity making the world a more interesting place to be, what really needs to happen is the element of being constant. I do want to be careful here because inevitably people think that means operating at 100 per cent for 100 per cent of the time, when in reality an 80/20 split is a better result mentally and physically, in all aspects of life. You can make life more interesting, open up more opportunities and possibilities – and maybe invent the next best thing by seeking to be constantly curious. The great thing about being curious is you don't even have to know what it is you are being curious about; just the act of asking questions and getting new answers will sit in your mind and one day will be there to be called upon. Just like the slow-burning inventions that were thought to be light-bulb moments, any information you gather could be useful when you least expect it. If you want explosive ripples, curiosity must come hand in hand with this.

Bringing it all together

Let's remind ourselves of all of the benefits of being curious:

- ➤ Curiosity is natural – but we're all curious about different things.
- ➤ Once you unlock it, it can unlock your passions and help every part of your life.
- ➤ Lifelong learning needs to be adopted as well as around-the-clock learning.
- ➤ Think about the importance of creating environments where hunches collide.
- ➤ Don't ever be brain lazy: try to find things out for yourself.
- ➤ Fearless curiosity is different to being reckless with your ideas.

Top tip: Think more like a child!

Be more toddler! What do I mean by this? It's not a case of being childish, but we can be more childlike – have fewer barriers, think less about the future and consequences, just getting on and giving something a go. Obviously this doesn't mean ignoring your responsibilities, such as bills or your dependents, but in situations where we can be more childlike we should be.

I have a toddler and when he has had enough of doing something he says, 'I've had enough, I want to go home', and we all know where we stand (and we know that trying to negotiate anything else with him at this point is futile!). On the flip side, when he gets in the washing basket and asks me to play trains with him, he genuinely believes it is a train and we are travelling somewhere; his imagination has no barriers, no one is telling him he cannot do something and he believes anything is possible. Wouldn't it be wonderful if we could take even ten per cent of this belief and imagination into our adult lives?

I once had a client project from a woman who ran a huge graduate scheme in a multinational organisation of 1000+ young people. She reached out to us and said that she needed help unleashing creativity from this cohort of employees. Her feeling was that these young adults, fresh out of university, were applying to her organisation using buzzwords to describe themselves as an 'innovator' or that they were incredibly 'creative'. In the first few months she would see this but, within three to six months, they were fading into being like everyone else in the organisation on the corporate treadmill and not coming forward with any ideas anymore – the spark had seemed to fade already. She wanted them to be more 'childlike' again and fearless with their suggestions. She wanted them to question the status quo and push the company forward. However, what was happening was that they were quickly blending into the background, which was the opposite intention of the scheme in this organisation.

We designed an incredibly creative programme with her and actually took cohorts of graduates into a school for a training session and would include children along the way. It was a remarkable programme. They would arrive at a school not knowing what they were about to do and were told we were using the school's hosting facilities for cost reasons. But within 20 minutes, 10-year-olds would be marching into the room and would be paired up with an adult to take part in a game. The 10-year-old and the graduate in a pair then had to work together on the task. It was genius! Not only was it fun and different, but as the morning unfolded and we blended seminars with activities with children, gradually the creative juices were coming back into these young people.

The key message and tip here is to think about how you can be more childlike from time to time. Don't put blockers up on your ideas even if they sound mad. As part of my work, I've worked with children as young as four who've invented with their imaginations – The Ever-Growing Shoe, the Animal Translator or the Fantastic Fridge. The shoe grows with your feet as you get old, the translator means you can speak to your pets and the fridge means you never need to go to the shops again – brilliant ideas. My advice is to get carried away with your imagination from time to time, or better still the imagination of children that you might be lucky to have in your life – your children, nieces and nephews, a friend's child, etc. Try to see the world from their point of view and just enjoy your imagination. Curiosity fuels creativity. Creative people make creative ripples.

Reflections

Remember those times as a child when being curious really was the most natural thing and even encouraged? Then over time you got older and were told not to get involved in things, not to ask unwanted questions, and the world wasn't very welcoming of the childlike innocent inquisitiveness. Instead it was easier to keep your head down and do what you needed to do, rather than perhaps what you wanted to do. But you have passions and you want to realise them. I want you to get that childlike curiosity back and use it to your advantage. You can be curious, you can be creative and you can be constant, and be all the better for it.

Curiosity has always helped me personally throughout my career and I continue to fuel it by making blocks of time at work where I can just think. Having a sensible work/life balance allows me a little separation to be able to come back to work with better ideas. I've even looked to occupy certain quiet times with fascinating podcasts from people I've never heard about to continue to learn. I've always found that my curiosity has led to me making new discoveries, new friendships and the creation of new ideas, which has helped my ripples spread further than I could initially imagine.

Takeaways

➤ Be a lifelong learner and never stop asking questions.

➤ Successful people will find different techniques to enhance their curious minds.

➤ Create the right conditions for being curious in the environments where you work.

➤ Be constant in your curiosity and creativity.

➤ Be more childlike – have fewer barriers and think less about the future.

Now it's time to look after the body!

Level 6

The Business Body

How can you possibly create ripples without having a healthy body and a healthy mind? Treat your body as an asset and it will keep you in good stead. Just as a business needs a strong foundation, good health will provide you with the foundation you need to be positively relentless and give you the edge you need every day. There is no point peaking once a week; that's not helpful because either side of that peak is an average you. You should be aspiring to make everlasting ripples every day, and your business body can give you the marginal gains you need to do that.

Have you ever thought about the phrase 'running a business'? The idea of running means something constantly moving and changing direction, being dynamic. We should connect this with the idea of keeping ourselves moving physically and emotionally.

It doesn't have to mean going for a run all the time, but any activity that gets you moving, clears your mind and focuses you will have direct benefits for you. This is what I want to explore in this level.

Healthy body, healthy mind

It's a long-standing belief that exercise has immense physical benefits, but what about the impact it has on the mind? A lot of research has been conducted examining the effect of exercise on children and education. A 2010 study by Aberdeen University, for example, showed that children who had '15 minutes of exercise in the classroom improved performance on cognitive tests conducted later in the day'.[29] It has similar effects on adults too; regular exercise leads to better concentration, being less inclined to be impulsive and instead being more thoughtful. Research also shows that exercise improves your brain in the short term by raising your focus for two to three hours afterwards.[30] That's an incredible statistic and demonstrates even more that our brains are muscles that need exercising to get the best out of them.

The science behind it lies with blood flow stimulating the brain's cells. According to the Dana Foundation, which researches the brain and health, 'These nourishing proteins keep brain cells (also known as neurons) healthy and promote the growth of new neurons. Neurons are the working building blocks of the brain. As a result, individual neuron health is important to overall brain

---

29 www.abdn.ac.uk/news/3600

30 Ratley, J. (2008). *Spark! The Revolutionary New Science of Exercise and the Brain*. Little, Brown.

health.'[31] It makes sense then that the best gift we give our children is teaching them from an early age about the benefits of leading a healthy lifestyle.

In my opinion the time dedicated to physical activity and exploring sports and games in schools, particularly primary schools, is just not enough. Once or twice a week isn't sufficient. It should be daily to help stimulate the brain, but more importantly give children exposure to many different sports to find something which sticks with them. I've always believed that there is a sport for every child and doesn't have to be just the mainstream ones of football, cricket, rugby, netball, hockey, etc. The Olympics and Paralympics are filled with fascinating sports which hardly any of us have ever tried and outside of these global games there are even more. Physical education in primary schools shouldn't just be about a carousel of sports, but offer an appropriate exposure to help a child find something which they're curious about and want to explore further themselves. If every child walked out of education with academic knowledge, knowing what their passions are and a sport or two which became a lifelong hobby, the impact on society could be way beyond imagination. It could help solve society's health challenges and many developing mental wellbeing ones because sport has the ability to help both of those areas equally. But it seems that most of us tend to learn about exercising later in life and are constantly playing catch-up with it.

With young children now, my wife and I are keen not to throw them into the sports we love but create that exposure for them at weekends and after school – to see

---

31 www.dana.org/article/how-does-exercise-affect-the-brain

if something sticks, particularly while they're in primary school. Our children have taken some enjoyment out of joining their parents out on a run, which obviously we love and they do too. I hope over the years they find a sport they are passionate about and give them as much as sport has given my wife and me.

When I think back, I remember as a teenager, I played every sport under the sun and loved it all, but most notably cricket, rugby and football in that order! It is part of my drive and pushing myself. For some children, however, doing physical exercise would be the worst thing in the world – but if you don't give them options and encouragement to participate, then of course it will be easier to sit out on the sidelines and make excuses. Just because not everyone is a natural sportsperson doesn't mean they should be exempt from keeping fit, and organisations and businesses need to consider what they can do to promote it too.

I speak often to people in my teams about the importance of breaking up the day and the fact that I never have any issue with someone exercising, going to the gym or for a run in the middle of the day if it's what helps them. I personally would normally have a 7–11.30 am period in the office and then go for a run, have a shower, a quick sandwich and get ready to go hard again in the afternoon and it would mean my productivity levels on either side of this were high. But there are also other things organisations can do, such as really promote the use of walking meetings, or encouraging phone call meetings again so people can walk home on the phone and get away from their desk. They can also encourage team meetings and social events to not always circulate around 'having a good time in the bar'. Don't get me wrong, I thoroughly enjoy these sessions, but it's not always the best philosophy or message to promote. It certainly doesn't promote healthy living and it can also alienate those people who don't drink or don't want to. It's not an employer's responsibility to take care of the physical fitness of its staff – that's down to individuals – but they can set the tone. By setting a good example and encouraging a healthier lifestyle, it not only helps the employee but it also drives energy through an organisation, which is often critical to its success.

Successful routines

When I was 27 I found that running had a positive impact on my day job and, up until that point, I had never run 10 kilometres despite a lifetime in sport. Running gave me the opportunity to not only stay in shape, but also run away from the noise of work. As my business began to grow, it was a stress reliever, an opportunity to not only think, but also learn with the rise of the business podcast. As finding time to read was becoming increasingly harder, listening to a podcast and to the premise of a book by someone being interviewed was perfect for me. So running had multiple benefits and I genuinely believe it helped save the business in the first year of the Covid-19 pandemic.

However, a story I must tell is that in 2020, during lockdown, my wife and I decided to run for 100 days in a row, for the equivalent length of Great Britain (1408 km), which was on average 7K a day each for 100 days. We did this for many reasons but mainly:

> ➤ we wanted to build up the foundation of our fitness for the challenges we were facing

➤ we needed the genuine space to work through some critical decisions, and
➤ to escape the noise of the house!

David Harkin
October 4, 2020 at 7:32 AM · Elmbridge, England

London Virtual Marathon - DONE

Congratulations, this activity is your longest run on Strava!

Distance	Avg Pace
42.52 km	4:51 /km

Moving Time	Elevation Gain
3:26:08	138 m

Calories	Max Elevation
4,304 Cal	40 m

View Analysis

Home Maps Record Groups You

As time went by, not only did I genuinely become the fittest I'd ever been (I ran my second marathon at the end of it and shaved nearly a whole hour off my first marathon time), but I made some of the best business decisions I've ever made.

In a VUCA world (Volatility, Uncertainty, Complexity and Ambiguity) and with a business under threat, I needed an escape to think. Our organisation at the time was a professional services company working in education. Within 72 hours, Armageddon hit. Every piece of work we had for six months was cancelled or postponed and a pipeline that was built up over the previous year was wiped. We went from a period of growth to one of survival. We went from green numbers on the profit and loss sheet to horrible red ones. We went from excitement to shock. Quite frankly it was horrific. There was, quite rightly, focus in the media on what was happening in hospitals and schools – this is exactly where the focus should have been.

However, millions of entrepreneurs and business owners around the world, who often had made huge sacrifices to create jobs for the economy, were in their own world of pain. You would turn on the TV and people would say 'businesses are struggling' but forget that behind every business is a person or people. I can certainly say we were struggling to get to grips with everything that was going on along with everyone else.

It was on a run though that I found myself creating the strategy we needed and then scrambling for a piece of paper on my return to the house. I remember thinking that I didn't want all of our hard work to become a Covid story and our children would never even remember a business which had given us so much in our lives. It then occurred to me that the strategy had to be a fourfold approach:

- ➤ protect
- ➤ opportunity
- ➤ reflect
- ➤ bounce.

Protect the business at all costs. Do whatever it takes to make sure we come out the other side to be able to create jobs in the future. Make the difficult calls if need be and protect key talent.

To seek new **opportunities** and see the market with fresh eyes. Forget everything that we had ever done and think about what skills we had in the team to solve problems in a VUCA world.

I then knew that the dust would settle and **reflection** would be key. We needed to reflect on what we had built in the past and be honest about every part of the business. What did we love doing? What weren't we doing as well as we should? Make pledges to myself in our next level to be better.

And then finally, plan the **bounce** back. Get the energy to go again and be better than before. Have bigger ambitions, think with scale from the start and go and make a dent on the planet.

As you can imagine, fitness is now part of my everyday life and I will now see my body as not just a temple, but a business. And other leaders seem to be in the same boat. There is no way you can honestly be at the top of your game or give yourself the greatest chance of success if you don't take care of yourself. You might be brilliantly busy, but find that time! I don't just keep fit for the sake of the business, but selfishly for me, to learn through podcasts, have the energy for my family, relieve stress, solve problems and explore the world I live in.

Learn from the best

Many high-achieving CEOs and leaders take on their physical exercise the way they take on their businesses – they have a relentless drive to stay fit and healthy, which helps provide focus. Even some presidents have some interesting routines. Let's take Barack Obama's routine of five hours of sleep a night and then 45 minutes of exercise in the morning, six days a week, and no caffeine. Baroness Michelle Mone is even higher up in the exercise stakes – working out three times a day! Her advice is to treat your body the same way you would a business plan and she runs her mind and body like clockwork.

It doesn't have to be as intense as that or the high-impact gym workouts favoured by Apple CEO Tim Cook or

Citigroup CEO Michael Corbat – they follow the Spartacus workout, a circuit workout that was designed by Liam McIntyre who played Spartacus in a TV series – pretty intense by the sound of it. It could be yoga that helps bring your mind and body into balance like Hootsuite CEO Ryan Holmes practises. Perhaps you would favour editor in chief of *Vogue* Anna Wintour's regime of playing tennis before 6 am. If you are anything like LearnVest CEO Alexa von Tobel, you could even take your co-workers with you to a spin class!

It's surprising what you can learn about your co-workers when you work out together. A brilliant member of my business is a great runner. He knew I was keen and wanted to help me with my marathon training. Despite him being nearly 15 years younger than me and sometimes running backwards because he was so quick, the conversations on those runs are when he impressed me the most. His passions for work and life exploded out of him. His curious questions seem to flow all the time. I learned more from his stories and I enjoyed his company. It's just proof that working relationships don't just need to be developed in an office or an establishment like a pub. Sometimes – probably, in fact – the best environment is fresh air – a walk or indeed a run!

There may be many things that contribute to this kind of mentality, and I am not suggesting you follow the routines of politicians or entrepreneurs to the letter, but if we just take a fraction of these relentless states of mind, we could make big improvements in ourselves. Just increasing the amount of exercise, getting up a bit earlier (if you are an early morning exerciser) or scheduling some in during 'dead' time (when you might normally be flaked out on the sofa), or just adding some more movement during your day in the office (stairs instead of lifts or indeed a standing desk instead of a sit-down one), can help. But be sure not to let yourself stagnate; it's great to start small and increase, but don't make the mistake of making it easy for yourself. Developing positive ripples daily doesn't happen by getting into your comfort zone and staying there – you need to break down those barriers. Increasing your physical exercise is as much a mental barrier as a physical one!

Discipline and commitment

Perhaps you are thinking that it sounds great, but how do I get past that mental barrier? The actor Matthew McConaughey was interviewed for Jake Humphrey's *High Performance Podcast* about how he manages to maintain his high levels of fitness. He cited *discipline* and *commitment*. The act of commitment is the same, regardless of your background or situation. What keeps McConaughey committed is the embarrassment he would feel by not being able to do his job properly if he lost his level of fitness.

You can think of this in the same way as your contribution to your day job. What would your personal embarrassment be if you didn't maintain your commitment to your personal goals? Making the goal isn't difficult or where the problem lies, but keeping to it is. This is where, as McConaughey would say, it becomes *non-negotiable*. You cannot give yourself the option of not doing it. So, when you're dusting off your trainers and getting ready to head out, and the voices in your head start trying to distract and detract you from the end goal, you need to be forceful and tell yourself *it's non-negotiable*. He calls it having a 'healthy obsession' and this is the one area where you can be a perfectionist.

It's not going to be easy and it isn't supposed to be.[32] Like I have said before, the end result will be all the better for it if you committed and knew how hard you had to work to get there. For example, you would never regret a run! After the initial period of recovery, the body begins to feel great, and that includes your state of mind.

Sluggish Tuesdays

With these examples in mind, I want to give you this real-life story of why it's important to keep yourself focused whatever day of the week. I call it 'Sluggish Tuesdays'. It's very easily done: the children would finally be quiet on a Sunday afternoon watching a film on the sofa, and my wife and I would have a glass of wine or a beer. It's that relaxing feeling you have as you've begun to unwind from Friday into the weekend and before the craziness of the new week is about to begin. But I realised that glass or two wasn't helping me at all as I kicked on into the working week. Alcohol, no matter the amount, impacts your sleep and your attitude the following day. That little Sunday evening drink would actually put me under more pressure on a Monday because the pace of my Monday was the same as every other day in a week – *positively relentless*. You can't lead a positively relentless life and be even five per cent sluggish; it's impossible. By Tuesday, my slight sluggishness would turn into my being a little bit 'short' occasionally, and I believe it was all linked to that glass of wine as the kids were watching *Monsters Inc* for the 100th time. I've now adopted the rule of not even a spot of alcohol on a school night if I want to be at the top

---

32 https://podcasts.apple.com/gb/podcast/matthew-mcconaughey-looking-for-lifes-green-lights/id1500444735?i=1000500730520

of my game for the five working days of the week. I owe it to myself, to the business and my team to be at the top of my game at all times.

And it's not just alcohol which has this effect on your body but obviously your food and calorie intake. I'm still surprised at how many people have no idea how calories work. Eating considerably more calories on a daily basis than you need will add to an increase in weight and sluggishness over time, but even just a couple of 'big' calorie days will lead to sluggish days in the week.

I wasn't a major calorie counter until someone told me how many calories were in a bottle of Lucozade and I fell off my chair. I knew a man should roughly consume between 2000 and 2500 calories a day but I didn't know until then that in one 500 ml bottle of Lucozade alone there are 310 calories. I was shocked and would look at the label and think 'How?'. The amount of sugar was the problem (estimated to be four teaspoons) and I was always a little more cautious from that moment onwards, glancing at the number when I picked it up off the shelf. I found the small decisions sometimes are just enough to really help you. For example, changing from drinking a cappuccino to a white Americano is about 175 calories fewer (depending on size and retailer, etc.). It might seem small, but over a year that's 63,875 calories – the equivalent of 32 days of calorie intake. Quite remarkable. It doesn't mean I don't have a cappuccino occasionally; it just means I don't treat myself all the time and also helps me to feel less sluggish. Sluggish Tuesdays were the result of not properly taking care of myself.

Sleep and the body

For Arianna Huffington, the co-founder of the *Huffington Post* and an influential speaker and author, her epiphany 'came in the form of a broken cheekbone and a nasty gash over her eye — the result of a fall brought on by exhaustion and lack of sleep.'[33] She had been neglecting herself, leading to burnout and stress. She is now passionate about the benefits of sleeping well and has written her own book on the subject – *The Sleep Revolution*. This sits well with the studies around exercise fuelling not only our minds and bodies, but also promoting better sleep, which then leads to better focus as well.

I've always been fascinated at how the topic of sleep is not a mainstream subject at school. School is about preparing you for your life and we sleep for six to eight hours (if we're lucky!) every day of our lives, but we don't teach people how to sleep. We don't study it at school. We don't see how we can improve it and leave everyone to try and work it out for themselves, but so many of us have sleeping issues. I'm not suggesting it should replace maths in the classroom, but a weekly or monthly deep dive into it, with students trying different techniques as they get older, could actually put them in a great position for the rest of their lives.

It is estimated that over 80 per cent of the world's population want to improve their sleep. Someone once mentioned the military method to me, which maybe we should have all been taught:[34]

---

33 www.ariannahuffington.com/thrive

34 From www.independent.co.uk/life-style/fall-asleep-fast-sleep-trick-military-b1912422.html

➤ Relax your entire face, including the muscles inside your mouth.

➤ Drop your shoulders to release the tension and let your hands drop to the side of your body.

➤ Exhale, relaxing your chest.

➤ Relax your legs, thighs, and calves.

➤ Clear your mind for 10 seconds by imagining a relaxing scene.

➤ If this doesn't work, try saying the words 'don't think' over and over for 10 seconds.

➤ Within 10 seconds, you should fall asleep!

This is the technique used to help tired individuals on the front line get to sleep quickly when they might only have a few minutes. A slight sidestep but hopefully of interest!

Know what works for your work life and your home life. I make sure that my relaxation doesn't negatively impact the rest of my working week. You need to judge your own feelings, situation and environment to know how relentless you can be and what kind of person you want to be every day of the week.

Mental wellbeing

This level can't be complete without touching on the mental wellbeing of an individual in helping you with your search of developing a business body. This is obviously crucial for so many different reasons. Fitness is not just physical; it's also your mental fitness and emotional fitness to be able to see things and handle challenges that you will face in your day-to-day life. I won't explore that in detail here because there are so many people better positioned out there to really help you if this is an area you're curious about – but what I will say, and what I believe, is a healthy body helps with energy, confidence, stress, anxiety and attitude, which surely must directly impact the mind.

First and foremost, apps like Headspace (even the NHS prescribes it) and Calm are hugely popular; and Brene Brown, Nedra Glover Tawwab, Matt Haig and Lori Gottlieb among others have done fantastic work in this area. Here are a few snippets of their wisdom:

➤ 'Between stimulus and response there is a space. In that space is our power to choose our response. In our response lies our growth and our freedom.'

➤ 'Most big transformations come about from the hundreds of tiny, almost imperceptible, steps we take along the way.'

➤ 'The things we protest against the most are often the very things we need to look at.'

— Lori Gottlieb, *Maybe You Should Talk to Someone: A Therapist, Her Therapist, and Our Lives Revealed* (Scribe, 2019)

➤ 'Wherever you are, at any moment, try and find something beautiful. A face, a line out of a poem, the clouds out of a window, some graffiti, a wind farm. Beauty cleans the mind.'

➤ 'The key is in accepting your thoughts, all of them, even the bad ones. Accept thoughts, but don't become them. Understand, for instance, that having a sad thought, even having a continual succession of sad thoughts, is not the same as being a sad person. You can walk through a storm and feel the wind but you know you are not the wind.'

— Matt Haig, *Reasons to Stay Alive* (Canongate, 2015)

> ➤ 'The ability to say no to yourself is a gift. If you can resist your urges, change your habits, and say yes to only what you deem truly meaningful, you'll be practising healthy self-boundaries. It's your responsibility to care for yourself without excuses.'
> — Nedra Glover Tawwab, *Set Boundaries, Find Peace: A Guide to Reclaiming Yourself* (Piatkus, 2021)

Bringing it all together

I don't expect everyone to be joining the gym following this, but hopefully it will give you a new appreciation for the body and how it really can impact your ability to make positive ripples.

- ➤ A healthy body and a healthy mind go hand in hand.
- ➤ Routines play an important part in creating new habits.
- ➤ Read up on what your role models have done to inspire you and consider what you can do.
- ➤ Be disciplined and committed to your body.
- ➤ Avoid sluggish days by considering what you eat and drink.

Top tip: Get on Strava and create your goals

Along with business goals, I also have personal health goals – more than I've ever had in my life. When I was a teenager, I never tracked my health or fitness to the level I do now – I think this is because it's something you just take for granted as a young person. My goals for my health aren't about losing weight or being a certain amount of kilos, but are now related to how I feel and general fitness. Using apps like Fitbit and Strava were turning points for me, particularly the latter. The information that I would get from Strava for 'Personal Bests' just unleashed a beast in me that there was always a PB to be working towards (a good example of my relentlessness), but I love it. Each quarter, there is a new PB I want to improve on: 5K, 10K, 10 miles, half marathon or a marathon, and the feeling is amazing when you do it; it has such a knock-on impact on work. You feel on top of your game as you run your quickest ten miles or shave two seconds off your 5K PB. If you're goal setting, or doing your Christmas CV for next year, you have to have healthy goals too, and don't make them weight related. Make them something different and there is always something more to strive towards. This reaffirms what was referred to by McConaughey about a healthy obsession. It's something that is always in me and I need to find an outlet for it in the best way possible.

Give it a go and create your own personal health goals. You may have to try a few things before you know what makes you 'tick', especially if you are new to doing this or have only stuck to one kind of exercise. The gym is great, but what about team sports or getting outside? But if the gym is working for you then stick with it, but keep making more goals for yourself. The pursuit of a world-class mind is about setting those long-term goals and not just sitting pretty once reached.

Try answering these questions to get you started:

1. What is one thing you want to improve on?
2. What stops you from moving on with this goal?
3. Do you feel fit in mind and body?
4. How active are you daily/weekly?
5. What words can you take from this level to help you achieve this goal?

Go set your goals, go make yourself accountable to yourself via a fitness app and make it happen. Right now, my physical goals this year are:

➤ get a marathon PB
➤ break a 20-minute 5K
➤ complete an ultramarathon

Reflections

If you want to make positive and even explosive ripples in your life, start by taking care of yourself. I think I always took it for granted until the most recent few years of my life. I was always fit and always bouncing off the walls, but as you become older it does get harder.

Takeaways

➤ Exercise and good health improve your cognitive abilities.

➤ Alcohol, even small amounts, affects your sleep and energy levels, so consider when you drink to stay alert on the working days of the week.

➤ Many of the world's best-known CEOs and leaders prioritise their health – so should you.

➤ Create personal health goals alongside your business goals every year.

Level 7

The Resilience Bubble

It's incredibly important, perhaps now more than ever, to surround yourself with people who have a positive impact on your life, people who add value and who will help you to be resilient when required – this is your resilience support group. But you should also consider every difficult moment in your life as building your own resilience bubble which doesn't ever get smaller, just bigger. That bubble will end up protecting and helping you no matter what you face in the future.

Resilience is the new buzzword in schools and businesses – but have you ever actually stopped and thought about it? This level is designed to dive into the whole theory of resilience, where you build it up from, how it can never become less over time and how it can help you build confidence with the more ambitious ripples you want to achieve. Time for Level 7...

Types of resilience

Before we dive deep into this level, it's important to distinguish the different types of resilience that exist and what I'll be referring to at different points. I'm not going to overcomplicate this, and will keep it to three: physical, emotional and professional. Let's begin with physical resilience.

Physical resilience is the ability of the body to withstand strain – the type of resilience that you need to complete a 5K, cycle across Britain or swim a few lengths in the pool. Personally, I've found myself wanting to test my body more as I get older and see how resilient it actually is. I mentioned earlier my interest in running has grown in the last few years and without a shadow of a doubt, completing a marathon is probably the most strain I've put on my body. The first time I did it, the weather here in the UK went from below 10 degrees to a staggering 27 degrees in a matter of days. It surprised every athlete on that day and hit me for six as I was running because all of our training was in sub-10 degrees temperature and at times it was nearly below freezing. I knew within minutes of starting that marathon that my target time would never be hit, but it was the last six miles where my body had to really dig deep to complete it.

Fast forward a few years and I've now been lucky to complete a marathon a number of times. Each time it becomes easier and my body has become accustomed to the training and challenges of a marathon. A friend who was big into their marathons once said to me, 'David, you need to normalise running 30K in your training, then doing the final 12K on the day will make it a breeze.' I laughed it off, but knew exactly what she meant, and in time my body just learned how to deal with that distance and it adapted. Nowadays, on my runs when I go that distance, I just want to get 10K in the bag because it feels good; 10–20K seems to go relatively easily as I'm in the swing of it; and then it's when I hit 20K I feel like the run is only about to get started. Your mind and body end up getting used to it and chunking it down into segments and sections. With each section complete, you give yourself a pat on the back and you crack on with the next stage. Each difficult training run and each marathon leads to my physical resilience bubble getting bigger. In the years ahead, I can now imagine myself aspiring to do an ultramarathon, which is typically 50–100K running, as I seek a new challenge to keep pushing myself and keep expanding that bubble. If you had said that to me 10 years ago, I would have laughed.

Then there is **emotional resilience**. This ability for the mind to withstand strain or stress put on it. Emotional challenges can come from every angle in your life. Emotional resilience is tested when family and loved ones are ill, when financial challenges come and surprise you, or when circumstances in your day-to-day life change dramatically. Emotional challenges are exactly that – emotional. The worst for me is when my loved ones are being affected – you feel your world is being pulled apart for something you can't control or worse still can't explain. Emotionally, I was probably tested the most when our son Harry was born. He arrived blue and with the umbilical cord wrapped around his neck four times. He was whipped away from us in seconds and taken to the emergency unit. Emotionally my thoughts were all over the place and I went from an immediate reaction of complete panic to my logical side kicking in, sourcing and searching for information in any way I could about our little boy. When he was taken away he hadn't been named yet. My wife and I had the name down to two if it was a boy. I feared the worst and couldn't have them just refer to him as 'Baby Harkin' so, as they were storming out of the room calling him that, I shouted, 'His name is Harry.' I then remember them rushing him down the corridor, calling him Harry, and I hope it helped a little bit in his recovery. After a few scary hours, we were finally allowed to see him and then hold him, but my emotional resilience was sorely tested. I do believe, though, that each time you go through a situation, your experience grows and so does your resilience bubble.

Then there is **professional resilience** – the strain that your work and career put on your body and your mind. In a world which is now 24/7 with emails on your phone, more Zooms in a week than you can ever imagine, and with colleagues on your social media platforms, it's getting near impossible to get away from work or indeed the challenges you face. For me, the most challenging times in my career have been leading a business through a pandemic, but that experience made me a better leader. With every small or big challenge, I find now that very little surprises me and my resilience bubble has increased.

There was also a moment in my career before becoming an entrepreneur which stands out. When I was in the corporate space, they had a very systematic approach to promotions. You had to pitch why you felt you should go to the next pay band to a room full of senior people. The more senior the band, the more senior the people. I knew I was ready to go for the next band. I was flying at work, pushing the boundaries of innovation and clearly delivering – but it would mean I would be the youngest person in the world on that banding, and I knew that people in that room who would have to approve it would know that too. I was up for the challenge.

I had the perfect presentation, with depth and good reasoning, and was ready to deliver it. Everyone before me or after me went through the same process: pitch for 15 minutes and then get 15 minutes of questions. However, as soon as I started, I got told to close my laptop and that they would be going for 30 minutes of questions – tough questions, unfair questions, questions which overstepped the mark. They certainly did that and, to be honest, they were bang out of order. They made unfair accusations in an effort to 'test' how I reacted. I realised I was in a professional fight and I stood my ground. But I also knew I was getting different treatment because of how young I was. My professional resilience was growing as it became a boxing match but I stood firm, and at the end of the 30 minutes I was told to leave. I left the room feeling angry and actually disappointed in the 12 vice presidents in the room. I thought to myself, I don't actually want to be like any of them or be in their shoes if that's the way they treat people. It was their way of testing me but the insults, false accusations and other poor tactics didn't really test me – they just annoyed me, and it was the final nail in the coffin of me making a decision. It wasn't the place I wanted to be if that's how I was going to end up. The following day, I was promoted and was put on a director's path. The same day I resigned and became an entrepreneur. They had not only built my professional resilience up, but within those 30 minutes made me ready to back myself and build a business which would make an impact on the world.

Whether it's physical, emotional or professional resilience, each is grown over time, with new challenges or new obstacles. But each type of resilience just adds to the lessons of the past and each time I believe your resilience bubble grows. It's a big bubble around you which never gets smaller because it's impossible to unlearn situations, experiences or memories you've put your body through physically. This means that resilience can only grow over time and your bubble can only get bigger. This kind of mindset is unbelievable when you face challenges, because you know as an individual that when you come out the other side, your resilience bubble will have grown.

Reacting differently

We all react differently to different situations because our resilience bubbles are all different. No two people are the same and no two people have led the same life. But apart from all being unique, why do we react differently?

Dr Kenneth Ginsburg, a paediatrician and a human development expert, believes there are seven components that build up resilience:

- ➤ competence
- ➤ confidence
- ➤ connection
- ➤ character
- ➤ contribution
- ➤ copying
- ➤ control.[35]

The one which stands out the most for me is 'character', that ability to bounce back from a difficult

---

35 See Ginsburg's website, www.fosteringresilience.com

physical, emotional or professional experience. But the confidence element is not simply a trait that people either have or don't have: it involves behaviours, thoughts and actions that need to be learned and developed in every single one of us from an early age until our last days.

Resilience is like a muscle and, like muscles, it needs to be exercised and it will take time for it to develop. It's not something you can do an exam in or study to accelerate your learning – unfortunately you need to wait for the tests of life which are thrown at you. It can be frustrating for people wanting to prepare themselves for the future, but it is generally one of those things you can't rush. You can, however, probably prepare yourself for when those moments arise by just being more aware of how your body works, how the mind ticks and what it takes to progress your career.

Let me give you an example of an industry I know a huge amount about – education. Without a shadow of a doubt, one of the hardest jobs in the world is being a head teacher. It means you're responsible for everything related to your students, staff and parent bodies. This includes the education and safety of the people in the school; the development and wellbeing of your staff; the expectations and demands of your parent groups. On top of all of this, you're expected to be in control of the 'business' side of your school, while developing the strategy, engaging with your governors or board of directors and, at the drop of a hat, being prepared for an inspection from your local authority. In no other job in the world do you also have so much emotion under one roof and in no other job in the world can you be (on a daily basis) one knock on the door away from a pastoral care situation which disrupts your day or whatever was on your agenda.

It's for these reasons why progress in education is so slow. It's for these reasons that I've always believed that there should be a CEO of a school and a head of education to split the responsibilities; but the sector is no way near that as a norm. Therefore, you're expecting a new head teacher to step up from a previous role such as deputy head to suddenly be in charge of everything. Whatever qualifications they've got, whatever coaching they might have received, nothing will truly prepare them for that job – this is why you see their resilience bubbles expand immediately upon a new position and they often change in demeanour and manner because of the magnitude of the job. It's without a shadow of a doubt one of the most difficult jobs on the planet, but one which is a perfect example to demonstrate that you can't buy resilience before you do the job. You have no choice but to learn it when 'Head Teacher' is placed on your office door.

Building resilience

I can hear some of you shouting at me when you're reading this saying, 'David, I hear you; experience will give you resilience, but how can I prepare for these moments, how do I build it? Give me something!' Here are some ideas for you to consider and explore:

> ➤ Learn to relax. This isn't easy. I find this very difficult with the speed of my working world now, but having that ability to relax is a game-changer. Relaxing allows the mind to unwind and move from being 'IN' a situation to being 'ON' a situation. Many of us struggle with 'relaxing' as our minds are moving so fast all day, but if you can learn how

to do it, and even begin to learn to be more selfish at times looking after yourself, you should be able to relax better in the future, which will help when you need to be resilient. For me, I've become a better relaxer by controlling how much time I'm on my phone!

➤ Practice thought awareness. Thought awareness is the process by which you observe your thoughts and become aware of what is going through your head. The first time I heard about this was actually via cricket. When a player is at the crease, more often than not, they will get themselves out with an incorrect shot, listening to the opposition or the crowd, or creating a situation in their head which doesn't exist. Some of the most talented players in the game never make it to the top because they can't control the thoughts in their head when they're batting. Try to stop and get aware of what is going through your head. See if you can create a trigger, which allows you to be 'ON' your thoughts and not 'IN' them. It's a remarkably hard thing to do, but in a moment or period where resilience is needed, this could help your decision making and give you a sense of perspective.

I remember speaking to a friend who loved to do the most challenging physical challenges. He had cycled across South America and had run across Iceland in world record times. He would tell me about the adventure and the stories, and one time we did a training session together. This man was uber fit and much younger than me. As he was killing me in some sprints, he explained that his psychologist, who was helping him with the world records, would constantly tell him about the importance of mind over matter, that the brain wanted to give in when you actually were only at 25–30 per cent capacity. It wanted to stop because it was trying to protect you, and he had learned ways of overcoming this. He learned about 'thought awareness' and it put him in good stead with dealing with his world record attempt.

> ➤ Finally, build your own self-confidence. When difficult periods face us, the body can be tested physically and emotionally. All sorts of thoughts will go through an individual's head, and in the toughest situations doubt could creep in. This is totally natural. Doubt creeps in because you've yet to go through the situation ahead of yourself. You don't know if you can do it. You don't know if you'll come out the other side. But you will. However, to give you more confidence beforehand, you can continue to build your own self-confidence in your ability. This isn't about being arrogant and feeling invincible in tough moments, but a realisation that you're going into a situation with experience, different levels of success and an optimistic mindset that you will come out the other side. Dust down your CV or LinkedIn profile and remind yourself of all of your achievements in the chapters of your life, in your working world and outside of it. Make sure it's there in black and white on these profiles and give yourself a pat on the back. These are little techniques I use with team members when they're a little down or low on confidence – I get them to go and do this reflection exercise to build them back up.

Be aware of your bubble

The buzzword of resilience has been around for many years, but no doubt accelerated in the Covid pandemic as resilience was shown by every person on the planet. Our way of life was challenged. Armageddon hit businesses. Hospitals were overrun. Schools changed. Civilisation as we knew it changed overnight and nations around the world went through multiple lockdowns.

As we moved between these lockdowns, we all learned to cope. It didn't mean we weren't frustrated or wished for a better day, but after the first lockdown, we created new routines to muddle through. As we moved from the second to the third, our resilience bubbles got bigger as our perspective and experience of the situation grew. We all became more educated about what was happening globally. We all got a new perspective on how important our health was. We all got more time to think than ever before, with fewer distractions and less time going out. This is still the case even for people running businesses from their homes and dealing with home schooling, which was our little challenge in the Harkin household. However, as time went on, nothing could surprise any of us and our resilience bubbles grew. When nothing surprises you, this is when you know your bubble is pretty big!

The same bubble grows as we enter the world of work. Very few of us get that first job with our first application and our first interview. Why? Because normally the jobs you apply for at the beginning aren't right for you; you have no interview experience and you have no idea why you're even being asked questions. However, after you begin to go through knock-backs, you begin to question exactly what you want. The rejections lead to new focus and then, eventually, you submit the perfect application and complete the perfect interview which lands you that job. The whole process of landing your first job is a great example of your resilience bubble developing and growing over time.

For me, resilience can never go backwards. You might have a knock, but every day you're building your emotional, physical and professional resilience. You're taking tiny steps in building up your bubble until you hit a moment where you see it accelerate quickly because your body is going under strain, your mind is being tested or professionally, you're being challenged. Your resilience never goes backwards – your bubble will only get bigger!

Being aware of your resilience bubble and of what you've learned over time will continue to give you confidence. This confidence and this bubble will help you create positive ripples and lock away those negative or toxic ripples. This is so important. Why? Because in these moments of real tests, particularly professionally and emotionally, this is when others will look to you. They will look to see how you're reacting. They will look for guidance and support to help themselves through the challenges you're facing. Releasing negative or toxic ripples at these exact moments is not what you want to do. You want to be able to get yourself 'ON' and not 'IN' the situation, to control your reactions and do your best to release positive ripples. Being aware of how big your bubble is already will no doubt help you at these exact moments.

Bringing it all together

This has the potential to be a deep level, one which makes you question how resilient you are. We're all resilient in different ways and we're all on a journey of developing that bubble. Let's remind ourselves of a few key things:

➤ There are lots of different types of resilience but we've focused on physical, emotional and professional resilience in this level.

➤ Resilience is built up over time with the 7Cs – competence, confidence, connection, character, contribution, copying and controlling.

➤ It's possible to accelerate your development by learning to relax, practising thought awareness and building confidence.

➤ Your resilience bubble will only increase over time and not get smaller.

Top tip: Know your bubble

I want you to do a reflection exercise and take it seriously. Stop and reflect on when you have to show significant resilience in your life to date, physically, emotionally and professionally.

This will help you build confidence, but it will also mean that you will never mumble an answer again when asked in an interview question around resilience. But go deep. Think hard and don't just go with the first thing that came into your head.

Personally, I would go through each of those three sections one by one and cover the whole of your life. Go back to the days when you were at school and into your childhood. Don't neglect these years because for many of us this is when the bubble might have accelerated the most.

When you do this exercise, write everything down and then stop and reflect and see which three made the biggest impact on you. I've shared snippets of these stories throughout this level and the book, but for me, this is how it works:

Professionally
➤ saving the business in 2020 in a VUCA world (see page 124)
➤ saving the business again in 2021 after a private equity deal fell through
➤ losing a multi-million-dollar deal at the very last moment early on in my career.

Physically
➤ running the London Marathon in 27° temperatures
➤ running the length of Great Britain with my wife over 100 days
➤ running a virtual marathon on my own in the rain in 2020.

Emotionally
➤ my wife having multiple cancer scares in her thirties
➤ our second child's scary start to life
➤ my own testicular cancer scares in recent years.

I'm sure my reflections will change over time, but as I wrote that list, it made me proud. It made me proud that I had given myself plenty of opportunities to challenge myself, have exposure to new opportunities and grow these aspects – particularly professionally and physically. But it also made me reflect on how far my bubble has expanded over time.

It doesn't mean I look forward to the difficult situations ahead, but it means I have greater confidence I can deal with them head on, and in those moments create positive ripples because I know how far my bubble has already expanded. Enjoy the exercise and I hope it gives you some greater confidence.

Reflections

Resilience can be knocked. Resilience will be tested. Resilience will come under attack. But you must remember, you *are* resilient. Your journey started as a child and your bubble exists.

Every opportunity or challenge is an opportunity to expand your bubble and where possible stretch yourself to give yourself greater confidence in the future. Your future self will thank you – always remember that pressure is a privilege in our life. Sometimes it can feel overwhelming, but pressure adds to our resilience as pressure is often created when we're pushing ourselves in every part of our lives.

The key reflection in this level I want you to take away is remember the bubble, and in those moments remember how important it is to be 'ON' and not 'IN' a situation to be able to create positive ripples and not negative ones. Now on to making your mark.

Takeaways

➤ Resilience isn't just about how you deal with hitting the wall in a marathon and having the physical resilience to push on: it's also emotional and professional.

➤ No two people react the same to a situation: all of our resilience bubbles are different sizes as we're all on different journeys.

➤ You can build resilience by learning to relax, practising thought awareness and building self-confidence.

➤ By simply being aware of your resilience bubble it will help in the future.

Level 8

Making Your Mark

If you throw a small pebble into a pond it will make its mark by making ripples. Every single day we have the opportunity to make our mark, and over a collection of days, months, years and decades we should all be proud to look back and see what those marks all added up to. Life is about grabbing and seizing every day. It's about building for our friends and family. It's about leaving the planet in a better place than how we found it. If we all made a concerted effort to make positive marks on this planet on a daily basis, then I know all the problems of the world would be solved. It's about taking responsibility, being aware this is down to you and making your mark by making positive ripples.

People shy away from the topic of legacy and making their mark. It's often something people say that they are not fussed about – but why? Why wouldn't you want to?

We should all be eager to leave our families, communities, schools, businesses, organisations and indeed our planet in better shape. In this level we will explore the topic of legacy and how you can make your mark by applying what you've learned through reading this book.

What's your legacy?

When we think about creating legacies, a weird but good place to start is by thinking about what people would say about you when you're no longer around. Let's take the eulogy at a funeral as an example. The eulogy is when a loved one will talk about that individual who passed away. They'll talk about passions, hobbies, professional achievements and accomplishments, and how much their friends and families loved that person. It's a summary of 10–15 minutes in length of how that person 'made their mark' on the planet – and then it's all over! An entire life is summarised in perhaps two or three thousand written words spoken by a loved one. But a eulogy should be more than a summary: it is an opportunity to inspire others as they listen and no doubt reflect on their own life and the ripples they make.

I remember my wife telling me about a funeral of a family friend that she went to. The man in question passed away not long after retiring and his eldest son spoke about him for 45 minutes, which is a little longer than usual. Less than 10 per cent of that time was actually about his work. The fact he was a CEO of a multinational firm seemed to merit a mere mention as his son talked about his love for sports, the clubs he was involved in and what a character and great father he was. For this man, his legacy was that he was a committed corporate worker, but the sports club he ran as a hobby was where his personality came out and where he made his mark inspiring thousands of children. I remember thinking how important it was therefore to do a job that was related to my passion and indeed have a balanced and fulfilled life.

As well as the lengthier eulogy, you have another chance to be remembered with an epitaph on a gravestone or an obituary printed in a newspaper. These are usually more succinct and can really sum up how that person has been most memorable. Take some of these famous epitaphs:

- ➤ Mel Blanc, the voice of so many cartoon characters, famously has 'That's All Folks' engraved on his headstone. It's not many words, but it certainly sums up what he left to the world.
- ➤ Bette Davis was a successful actress of her time but faced great struggles on the way – hers reads, 'She did it the hard way.'
- ➤ Martin Luther King Jr: 'Free at last, Free at last, Thank God Almighty I'm Free at last.'
- ➤ Martin Guy White, a marine biologist and diver: 'I travelled the world with work that I love.'[36]

It's things like this that might make us laugh, but they can also make us think, just like a eulogy where we reflect on a person's life. Yes, some of those names might be well known, but what is said after they have gone reveals even more, especially the last one – that really demonstrates someone who did something that they were passionate about, and that's what I keep wanting to reiterate to you.

The summary of your 'mark' doesn't have to just be your eulogy or gravestone, but might include your last school

---

36 www.legacy.com/advice/100-best-examples-of-epitaphs

report and the everlasting impression you left with your teachers; the speech from your former boss on your last day of employment in a business; or what your friends and family say about you and your attitude to life when you're not around. The impression you leave people is your personal brand. It's the mark you're leaving on others on a daily basis and I think it's important for individuals to reflect on it.

Some might turn their nose up at this point and say that they're 'not fussed'. But I'm sorry, I don't believe it for a second. I don't believe people who say they don't care what others think. They might not care what strangers think, but how can you not possibly care what your friends or family think about your attitude, approach and way of life? The truth is, we all care. We're humans with emotions and it's important to think about your legacy – not just on the planet, but the legacy you're leaving behind at every chapter of your life.

Create your legacy now

Why wait until you pop your clogs to have a befitting memory created for you? This is why I want you to start thinking about this now, and not let life pass you by before you have had a chance for a legacy to be created where you can actually hear how great people think you are! That does mean, though, *maintaining* a positive legacy too; it doesn't take much for a legacy to be tarnished. There are many examples in the business world where someone has fallen foul of this, and the outcome has meant that any of the good things have been overshadowed by a wrong decision or misbehaviour towards others.

A legacy can also be interpreted differently by people. This is why doing what you love has to be a distinguishing factor of your life so that you, dare I say it, die happy! If you are in a corporation or have your own business, what positive contribution do you want to leave behind? Glen Llopis' article in *Forbes*, 'Five Ways A Legacy-Driven Mindset Will Define Your Leadership', takes the words out of my mouth:

> *Legacy is not bound by age or time served. Legacy represents your body of work at each stage of your career as you establish the foundational building blocks and accumulate the required wisdom to contribute to growth, innovation and opportunity both in and outside of the workplace.*[37]

Interestingly though, I find people don't realise that legacy is left not just at the end of our life but also after every significant chapter, and so many people have no idea what they've left behind. Let me give you an example. I'm often asked to coach aspiring talents who are attempting to be leaders in their organisations. I often do my digging before I speak to them and start with LinkedIn. I look down their profiles, which are often weak, and beneath each previous position is often next to no detail. They might have worked for someone for five years and on their public digital profile on LinkedIn they have just a few bullet points. When I ask them about what legacy they left behind in that role, they pause and are never sure. When I ask them about their successes, they might tell me one or two. I then ask a question to get a deliberate reaction: 'Is that it? Are you telling me you worked for that organisation for five years and only did that?' The reaction is always the same, 'No David, I did lots,

---

37 www.forbes.com/sites/glennllopis/2014/02/20/5-ways-a-legacy-driven-mindset-will-define-your-leadership

I was also involved in XYZ' and then suddenly they start telling me about the employees they mentored, the social initiatives they started, the transformation programme they led and the charity fundraiser they started.

For the life of me, if these high fliers need a prod to remember it, how will the rest of us? I encourage them to think about their highlights behind the revenue numbers or productivity contributions they installed in their role, and have that collective set of achievements proudly on their LinkedIn profile. It's a way for them to remind themselves constantly of a legacy they have left at a previous organisation and it's a reminder to all of us when we think of that individual.

It's also about what the next generation is going to do after you. Any skill, trade or way of working has to be passed down to each generation, and each generation improves on it and leaves its own legacy in the process. No business can continue beyond the current leadership if the leader hasn't put a legacy in place. That's why I believe there is no place for complacency or an attitude of keeping those business secrets to yourself. We all have an expiry date (excuse the phrase!) and the sooner we understand this, and not only grab all the opportunities afforded to us, but ensure we bring people along for the journey, the sooner we can start to turn these ripples into legacies.

As Llopis says in that quote, there is no age or time set on when you can create a legacy. It doesn't matter how long you have been in a business or have been running one. The important thing is that you made some dynamic changes or left an impression, something people will remember you for and that will inspire them into action.

If we take sport, a great example of legacy is the All Blacks rugby team. They live by their 15 team principles –

all players are expected to pledge their allegiance to them. If you want to be on this team, you will play by these rules, and it's as much a set of rules for off the field as for on it. Their mantras carry weight in many other organisations which seek to emulate a similar environment for their employees, so they're worth paying attention to. Far from being restrictive or exclusive, it has a way of being inclusive: regardless of your background, the whole team is playing by the same set of mantras and there are no excuses (a feature that has cropped up before in this book).

I won't state every single team rule (although I would urge you to look them up though as they're well worth a read), but the three takeaways I want you to reflect on are:

➤ **'Pass the ball – leaders create leaders'** – in leaving your legacy, this is key. You need to learn how to share your knowledge and create leaders within your team.

➤ **'Be a good ancestor'** – leave your team in a better place for the person who follows.

➤ **'Write your legacy'** – the All Blacks get a gift of a book featuring shirts from legendary teammates which is given to each new player and includes blank pages for them to fill in. It sends a powerful message that regardless of what has gone before there is still history to be made. Build your legacy.'[38]

Sports teams in general are known for being driven and the 'jersey they now wear represents decades of previous sports legends who wore that very same jersey.

---

38 https://thewhitehorsefederation.org.uk/downloads/default/All-blacks-Poster_01.pdf

They're aware that the fans will now hold them to the very same standard that they held their predecessors'.[39] And the thing with competitive sports is that the shelf life is considerably shorter than in any other career, so it really matters to those players to do the best they can in the short space of time they have to do it.

These examples from sport show how cohesion in your team and strong values from the top down have a positive effect on all who are in it. What about responsibility though? Have you made it your mission to ensure you have good leaders in place in your organisation, ones who will continue your values and ethos that are the foundations of what you do? Do you encourage your team or those around you to think and reflect? Have you done this yourself recently? It's a powerful tool and sets up your world-class mentality – one driven by legacy.

Businesses are terrible at reminding employees of previous employees' legacies and this is why people always feel like a number when they leave, which is such a shame. I remember leaving my corporate job, albeit excited about becoming an entrepreneur, and thinking 'I know I made a dent, but no one will ever remember it in that business, or really care'. Businesses need to do more. When an employee joins my business, in the first few days I always make a point of speaking to them. My message is simple: *Be You, Be Curious, Be Innovative and Make Your Mark* on this organisation. Help our business be better tomorrow than it is today and help us with our mission. Otherwise, what's the point? I don't say that last part but I always make sure they know I want them to bring their personality into the heart of our business and really contribute.

---

39 www.sportsretriever.com/baseball/legacy-factor-success-sports-team

Part and parcel of a business is that people will move on and at that point, upon exit or in a team meeting, I will always thank them publicly, highlight their successes, make sure that they're proud of them and wish them all the best with the next journey. We will talk about the mark they made with a smile and remind everyone else that they're still on their journey of doing the same. It's a small step in the right direction, but I definitely think businesses can do more in helping employees make their legacies and know exactly what their impact was when they eventually move on.

Lead by example

A really positive legacy is left through people, not results. Of course it's great if you took the company to another level financially and hit monetary success, but in terms of what people will say about you, it will be about who you were, what you were about, the little things you did. Those things live on in people – the way you made them feel – so be careful that you are trying to leave a positive legacy behind and not a negative one! We all know someone who 'left' their workplace in hushed circumstances and their name was never mentioned again. When you want to really think about this legacy you are leaving, start modelling your behaviour to your employees so they can see what you do; practise what you preach, as it were. It is indeed the doing that counts the most. *You can't make ripples on the sidelines: you have to be in the centre!*

Within the book I have quoted many influential and inspirational people in history and this is because they have left a legacy. Great people like Martin Luther King Jnr, Marie Curie, Nelson Mandela, Mother Theresa and

Albert Einstein – they all left huge legacies, but these are just a drop in the ocean. What I have really been showing you is that there are different types of legacy and they are being created every day. And don't forget, the legacy doesn't have to be after you have left this mortal realm, it could just be when you have left a business and changed jobs! The best advice I can give you then is to *be your best self and do your best at all times*. If nothing else, you will be known for always being the one to try.

Sometimes, though, it's not just the memories you leave behind or impact; it can also be about the financial legacy that you leave on your loved ones. Over a period of a lifetime, people will accumulate their wealth which will be passed on and it's key to think about that. Think about the legacy you want from your wealth and make sure it's passed on properly or goes to good causes.

A quick look online reveals how many celebrities are refusing to leave any legacy of that nature to their children and instead expect them to be able to make it for themselves. Many believe that the silver spoon won't give their children the impetus to propel themselves to success. This is an interesting argument and one you can thrash out for yourself, but it certainly gives us another thought process on what legacy means to people and what they believe could be a negative one to leave for their children. This ties in with what legacy means for us on a mindful level – the determination and motivation to go out and make something happen. It is your mentality that you have to work with, so regardless of what you have or haven't been given, you have to make peace with that and make your ripples as you see fit.

You choose how you want this to be seen. To be able to do this, you need to look ahead. You can go about your day-to-day life; you can create a five-year business plan, but what is happening beyond that? Matthew McConaughey in his book *Greenlights* talks about seeing into the future. Often children can't see beyond the next five minutes; adults sometimes can see only the next year ahead, whereas some can see their whole life. To me, I can see my whole life and because of this, I know how I want to make my mark. I can see my whole life because I know exactly what I'm passionate about and therefore I'm fully committed and dedicated to it, which makes it easier. I want my loved ones to listen, to be inspired and then go and continue to make their own marks.

First and foremost, I want my mark to be on my wife and family – one where they're happy and fulfilled and my contagious energy rubs off on them so they can continue to explore their passions and hobbies. Second, I want the businesses that I create to have a huge impact and ripple on the world, whatever they might be. Lastly, I want to help shape the vision for education for generations to come to be inspired. If I do those three things, my mark will be made. It's about a can-do attitude, going above and beyond and goal setting. I have these statements on my noticeboard and I'm fully committed to achieving them.

Making your mark

You can either think this is a morbid way of living or a way of giving yourself structure for the rest of your life. You need to ask yourself: what do you want to be remembered for? How are you demonstrating that? How are you making your mark? This is where so many of us fall down; we can't or don't want to look that far ahead. It can be a scary thing confronting your own ending, but look at it another way, the people you still talk about, those inventors, game-changers, special people who walked here before us, do they not stay 'alive' because we are talking about them? Don't think of it as the end – it is merely the beginning and it's never too late to start.

Bringing it all together

As we move towards the end of the final level, I think it's important that we bring this one together and recap some key messages and takeaways from the book in general:

- ➤ Don't be shy on the topic of legacy: we only have one life, so let's make an impact.
- ➤ There is absolutely no need to just do this at the end of your life. We should be constantly thinking about the chapters of our lives and what we can do to leave one chapter in the best way before we move on to the next.
- ➤ Sport is not bad at doing this: one reason is that it's constantly in the public eye, but also coaches know the idea of legacy is the best way of getting performance out of a team. You've often only got a few optimum years and it drives high performers to their max. Maybe businesses and organisations can consider what they're doing more to help employees leave a legacy and not simply leave a business.
- ➤ Lead by example: you have to lead your own life, or your teams, in a way you'd like to see emulated. Be proud of what you're personally achieving. It's not about boasting, but recognising your life's contributions to society and being proud of them.

Top tip: Plan your legacy

I have given you some thinking points and questions to ask of yourself throughout this level and you may be thinking, 'How do I start planning a legacy?' It's a good question because in some ways it can be better that it happens naturally and organically; but I am making you self-aware so a starting point might be helpful.

Don't get too bogged down with what has happened before – let's start with a clean slate. You can make a plan just like you would a to-do list, or a business plan if you want to make it really detailed, and give yourself time frames to achieve things. Write down some promises to yourself that will also have a positive effect on others. You should also measure these successes – saying, writing and doing is brilliant, but you will need some way of measuring if these have worked. And above all else – never stop! Legacy doesn't end when you have written that list.

➤ Start with what is important to you (family, friends, colleagues, business, environment, education, etc.).

➤ Be honest with yourself – have you been your best self to all of these people/causes? If not, start to plan what you can do to be better. Do you need better communication, getting more involved, being more available, more acknowledgement of what people have done?

➤ Who inspires you and why? (Think about their achievements and why that matters. Are you trying to emulate that or maybe even better them?)

➤ Make a list of three things you think someone would say about you that you are memorable for or what you wish people would know you for (why not even ask people and see what they say?).

➤ What are your passions/hobbies? Do you share these with people around you so they know a bit more about you? Remember – having passions makes people connect with you. If you haven't got any, get involved with some. Go and make ripples in something.

➤ Think about yourself as a leader – and do you have like-minded leaders in your team? (If there are issues with leaders in your team, think about how the next point could help. Have you invested in their development with training? Can they approach you when they need it?)

➤ Are you mentoring anyone right now? If not, this would be a great place to start leaving your legacy. (This doesn't have to be the newest members of the team – think about the ones who have been with you a while, perhaps they could do with some personal investment.)

If you're struggling with the above, maybe a good way to start is by looking at what you've achieved in every part of your life. Your work. Your hobbies. Your family. Update your LinkedIn profile and give yourself a pat on the back. Come back to these questions and then go plan your legacy in these areas for the years ahead.

Reflections

Sometimes it's easy to forget how privileged we are to create a business and run it, to be employed in a team and contribute, or to be part of a club or society and enjoy it. Whatever your role in life is, whatever you spend your time doing, there is always a way to contribute and make your mark. In your big areas of focus, which might be your family and your career(s), don't be ashamed of it. Think about the mark you're leaving and don't leave it too late. Every day is an opportunity to shape your contribution, make the world a better place and be a good person. Consider your legacy today and what you want it to be in the future – and go and make your mark, which in turn will help you make those positive ripples on the planet.

Takeaways

> ➤ It's never too early to start planning your legacy – how you'll be remembered is down to you.
> ➤ A legacy isn't just created after you have left this mortal realm; it could just be when you have left a business and changed jobs!
> ➤ The best way to create a positive, lasting legacy is to *be your best self and do your best at all times.*

Concluding Words

You made it! Thank you for sticking with me. You can give yourselves a big pat on the back.

I wrote *The Ripple Effect* to take you on a journey to realise how powerful your attitude is to the ripples you make on others on a daily basis, but now it's down to you.

I passionately believe that we're living in a world of exciting opportunities. Every single day around us, we have the opportunity to connect and make ripples far beyond what we can imagine. Being aware of them now will put you in good stead for your future.

It is never too late to start afresh and implement what you want from this book. Out of the 40,000+ words, there might be one or two points, tips or reflection moments or a story which really resonates with you and helps you with your day-to-day goals. If that's been achieved, then perfect.

Whether you've read this on a sun lounger, commuting to work or indeed in bed, I hope you take something away.

I'm certainly not perfect. I certainly haven't built a

unicorn business or won an Olympic medal. But I'm a normal person with big ambitions, who is a glass-half-full person and knows how important attitude has been to me so far. That attitude has allowed me to get to where I am in my career and I'm proud of that – but I have plenty to do:

➤ I know I must continue to be positively relentless.
➤ I know I must continue to be brilliantly busy doing what I love.
➤ I know I must learn from failures to make longer-lasting positive ripples.
➤ I know how important curiosity will be to future adventures.
➤ I know that I must look after my business body.
➤ I know that my resilience bubble will never get smaller, which gives me great confidence.
➤ I know I have a duty to leave my mark on my family, friends and the world.
➤ I know I must go and create some more exciting ripples.

Good luck in making your positive ripples in the days, weeks, months and years ahead. It is surprising how small changes can lead to big things and these tips I've shared have had a dramatic impact on me. Always remember, if you throw a pebble into a pond, it will always make ripples – and every day, so will you. I'm looking forward to building on these in the future, and indeed the opportunities ahead. Now it's your turn!